BILLY
GRAHAM
Evangelistic Asso

Always Good News.

SO-AWZ-223

Dear Friend,

I am pleased to send you this copy of *Praying for a Miracle*, by Don Wilton, senior pastor of First Baptist Church in Spartanburg, S.C., founder of *The Encouraging Word* broadcast ministry, and frequent speaker at the Billy Graham Training Center at The Cove. This gifted Bible teacher also served as my father's pastor. In my father's later years when his health kept him at home, Don Wilton faithfully visited with him nearly every week.

In *Praying for a Miracle*, Pastor Wilton invites you to discover the Biblical basis for our belief in miracles—supernatural events that only God can perform. Explore Jesus' first miracle recorded in Scripture and then study how you can seek the Lord's guidance, power, and will in your own life. I pray that this book will encourage you and deepen your understanding of Jesus' words in Luke 18:27 *"the things which are impossible with men are possible with God"* (NKJV).

For more than 65 years, the Billy Graham Evangelistic Association has worked to take the Good News of Jesus Christ throughout the world by every effective means available, and I'm excited about what God will do in the years ahead.

We would appreciate knowing how our ministry has touched your life. May God richly bless you.

Sincerely,

Franklin Graham
President

If you would like to know more about our ministry, please contact us:

IN THE U.S.:
Billy Graham Evangelistic Association
1 Billy Graham Parkway
Charlotte, NC 28201-0001
BillyGraham.org
info@bgea.org
Toll-free: 1-877-247-2426

IN CANADA:
Billy Graham Evangelistic
  Association of Canada
20 Hopewell Way NE
Calgary, AB T3J 5H5
BillyGraham.ca
Toll-free: 1-888-393-0003

Praying for a Miracle
Impossible Things Made Possible

don wilton

This *Billy Graham Library Selection* special edition is published with permission from Deep River Books.

©2012 by Don Wilton. All rights reserved.

Deep River Books, P.O. Box 310, Sisters, OR 97759

ISBN 978-1-59328-621-7 (BGEA Edition)
ISBN 13: 978-1-4141-2229-8
ISBN 10: 1-4141-2229-2
Library of Congress Catalog Card Number: 2011919272

Contents

Praying for a Miracle

Don Wilton

John 2:1–11

THIS BOOKLET IS about miracles. I am writing about these things because so many of us need a miracle, or two, in our lives. Most of us need many of them because life presents one challenge after another. One lady told me she would need a miracle to take place in order for her marriage to stay intact. Another young mother was told she could never have children of her own. And yet another had sent out over 700 resumes in an effort to find work and believed only a miracle would allow him to provide adequately for the needs of his family.

Miracles happen! I believe this. I do not believe the age of miracles has passed by for the simple reason that God is still very present in our world and very actively engaged in the affairs of people like you and me. Because of Him, miracles have happened, do happen, and will continue to happen. But they may not be what we have made them out to be. In fact much of the truth about miracles has become distorted and the very substance of these wonderful demonstrations of the power of God have become lost in mountainous seas of preacher talk and wishful thinking. As the years have rolled on by, the church, preachers and priests, lonely people, sick people and desperate housewives have all called for or claimed various brands of miracles. Everything from abuse to neglect, fringe theology and fund-raising pretenders have clamored to claim a corner on something that can only belong to the heart of God. Certainly, by definition, some can claim an inevitable miracle that caused them to be in the right place at the right time, but in order for something truly miraculous to take place, God has to be involved all the way.

So, the simple question is, "What is a miracle?" What does the Bible have to say about this? Surely God's Word is the only place we can search to find the truth because it is truth. All of the Bible is true in every way. It is absolute truth. It has no mixture of error. It is not some ordinary book written with the purpose of offering a few insights and suggestions to people. What God says in His book comes from God alone. So, let's go to God's Word and discover what He has to say to teach us about miracles.

Your life is very important to the Lord Jesus Christ. He wants the best for you and will always work His will in you. So, before despair sets in let us consider some important facts related to miracles.

We begin with three facts about miracles. First, miracles are something only God can do. Otherwise it is not a miracle. Good decisions are possible to make just as the correct medicines can be given to fix a wide assortment of physical problems. There are many times you and I do not feel well, for example, and we end up going to the pharmacy to pick up our doctor's prescription. The medicine works and we are healed. This is wonderful but this is not necessarily a miracle. God has given us common sense and very good doctors to take care of us. And He can work miracles through our doctors—so let's not get ahead of this first fact about miracles. If you can do it or cause it or bring it on, then God has

3

answered your prayers. Perhaps He has used that doctor or that friend—or simply your plain common sense. So, it went well and you passed the test and made it through, for which all of us can rejoice—but what happened was just good sense, clear thinking, self-discipline or something falling in line at the right time and in the right place.

A miracle is something much more. It is miraculous! Let me use two illustrations.

The first is an example of the real blessings of God and, certainly, answered prayer. When I developed a blood clot in my shoulder several years ago, the Lord answered the prayers of many people who love me and interceded for me. He used my doctors to eliminate the problem and He gave me enough sense to embark on courses of action to make certain this does not happen again. As I look back I give all praise and glory to the Lord because He answered our prayers. He blessed me. He worked through those who were qualified to diagnose and eliminate my health problem. In fact, I really believe only the Lord really knows if my situation could be classified as a miracle.

I believe this next example falls into the category of a miracle. When United States Marine 2nd Lt.

Andrew Kinard stepped on that monster in Iraq the blast threw him more than thirty feet up into the air. Both his legs were blown off and he suffered catastrophic injuries in every way. Together with his precious family, a large group of us gathered in the family home and cried out to God. We knew very little and had almost no information. Shortly after Andrew arrived at Bethesda I was privileged to be the first person to walk into his room, while his father, a highly skilled surgeon himself, waited anxiously outside his son's hospital room. What I saw tore my heart out. Let alone the massive injuries, Andrew was hardly recognizable as the vibrant and strapping young man I knew him to be. God gripped my heart intensely. I clearly remember crying out to the Lord—"Oh God, please do something! This is Andrew, Lord! I love him like a son. Besides he is Harry's son, Lord. If for no other reason Lord, do it for Harry and Mary! Lord, Andrew was serving our country. This whole family is faithful to you. Don't let him die Father! He's one of my son Greg's best friends. He has an incredible future. Father, please intervene and do something only You can do. Lord do a miracle in Andrew's life!!" I really do not remember everything I said to God that day, but I was joining with hundreds of people in crying out to the only one who could do something for Andrew. And He did.

As Harry entered the room and saw his son for the first time I knew God was in there with us. From within the unspeakable silence of a stunned father's heart and soul came the powerful presence of the only One who is capable of doing for us what we cannot do for ourselves.

By definition a miracle is a supernatural act requiring supernatural intervention. As Christians we believe only God can do for us what we cannot do for ourselves. If God HAS to be involved in order for it to take place—it can only be a miracle.

Second, miracles are impossible things made possible—only by the Lord Jesus, of course. Again, analysis of the event or happening should produce conclusive evidence that without God's intervention, what happened could not possibly have happened because it was impossible that it did happen! So, take any circumstance in life and ask this question, "Is what I need impossible to accomplish? Can anything human make this happen?" We will see this clearly in the miracle of Jesus when He changed the water into wine. Could a tablet, or a prescription, or a genius, change water into wine? So, miracles can only be defined by possible impossibilities.

Third, miracles are the "show and tell" of God's glory. In a sense they display God for the world to see. They are "bill boards" that contain "pictures" of the power of God to the point at which people are left in wonder and amazement at His goodness and loving care. It is through the means of miracles that our Savior demonstrates His ever-present compassion for His children and His abiding presence. They are designed by God for the benefit of His elect to show a lost and dying world that He alone is God. Miracles demean the notion that God has any rival and establish the fact that He does not share His platform of sovereignty with any other gods.

I have no doubt in my mind that there are many of us who are in desperate need of a miracle right at this moment. We are living in a rather precarious day and age, because the word "miracle" has become abused. Preachers have to exercise great wisdom when referring to others on television, but one only needs to turn on a television set, and it doesn't take long to find a "preacher" who is talking about miracles. You hear statements like, "Send your money, and receive this prayer cloth. If you will only pray with it, you will receive a miracle!" It's a catch-word in today's day and age. "Pay for it, pray with it—and see what God will do for you!" Sounds awful, doesn't it? But sadly true. Many of us have received e-mails instructing us to "Send this e-mail to 10 people and you will receive a miracle." This is not what I'm referring to in this booklet! Miracles come from God at His choosing, but often as the result of a deep and abiding relationship with Him!

Let's think about the wonder of miracles and all the Lord has in store for those who love Him. Others may not know what is going on in your life at this point, but certainly our Savior knows, and He wants you to be fulfilled in every way. You may need the miracle of healing in your body, healing of a relationship, or healing of your heart. You may need a miracle to pay your house payment for the next month. You may need a miracle to find a job in this economy. You may need a miracle to save your marriage, or you may need a miracle to overcome an addiction. Perhaps the son or daughter you love has broken your heart and you are praying for a miracle for your prodigal child to return home.

The Bible teaches us some rather extraordinary things about the issue of miracles. Personally I have become intrigued by the subject to the point that my faith and trust in God has been deepened. I have always known that our Savior does extraordinary things for those He loves, but, after studying the subject of miracles in the Bible, I now find myself praying for others with a far greater sense of expectation in my heart. God does perform miracles today. He will do so for you. I meet people on a daily basis who are constantly searching for miracles. I know a couple whose marriage is falling apart. A wife came to me just recently and said, "Pastor, only a miracle can bring my husband back home again." I've met many parents who have expressed the agony of their hearts concerning their sons and daughters. I would not be surprised if your heart is breaking because of a son, a daughter, or a grandchild, who is not living for the Lord. Maybe you know exactly when they made a decision for Christ, or possibly you wonder if in fact they really did, and you're asking God for a miracle. Not only do individuals or families need miracles, but there are many churches in dire need of a miracle as well. I know people who are praying for miracles in every kind of circumstance of life.

We will examine this subject together, and I believe that God's Word will make application by

His Spirit in your heart and life. I really believe that the Lord Jesus will do for you what you cannot do for yourself. I am praying for every person that reads this booklet! I pray that our Heavenly Father will reach down and touch your heart. I believe that's what God does when you ask Him!

"Our Father, we stand amazed in your presence, and we thank you for the inestimable privilege of knowing you as our Savior and Lord. Father, for just a moment, we would consider your Word, for we understand that your Word is a lamp unto our feet and a light unto our pathway. But Father, we are faced by this thing called life. We are praying, Father, for a miracle in our hearts! Lord, we are asking you to reach down from the portals of Heaven and speak to each and every heart within the context of their own circumstances. Father, we are always amazed, because your Word never returns void. Father, we bless your most hallowed name, and we consecrate our lives to you. Speak to us now as we study your Word. We pray these things together in that wonderful name, which is above every name, the name of our Lord and Savior Jesus Christ. Amen."

The First Miracle

I HAVE HOSTED many wonderful groups of people on trips to Israel for tours of the Holy Land. We visit many different places, but one of the most memorable places is in Cana of Galilee at an historic church called "The Wedding Sanctuary." There I am privileged to officiate at the renewal of the wedding vows of many of the couples in our groups. It is a meaningful experience for those who are involved, but unlike the weddings of Jesus' day, the ceremony only lasts for a short time and each couple is given a certificate commemorating the renewal of their vows before we move on to the next site.

In John chapter two we read the intriguing account of the first miracle Jesus performed in the same area in Cana of Galilee. History books suggest it was traditional during the time of the Lord Jesus Christ to have wedding celebrations that lasted longer than many of our Saturday afternoon weddings of today. They were extraordinary occasions. These happy gatherings were the social functions of the year, and everybody who was anybody received an invitation. In this case, Jesus was among the guests invited. The master of the ceremony usually served the best wine first. This was, most likely, according to the custom of the day. The limited numbers of vineyards in these regions usually meant it was better to serve the best wine when they all arrived at the wedding. The texture of the wine would have been at its fullest, richest and best. Perhaps it was also safest for the host to do this. We all understand the importance of first impressions. Besides, no father of the bride would want to embarrass his daughter at this show-and-tell moment of her life!

As time passed by supplies would begin to dwindle. In anticipation of the pending problem servants would be dispatched to wells with big water pots. Unlike some of the surrounding areas, Galilee was known for its fresh water—even though they didn't drink a lot of it, because it was unsanitary in many instances. What followed is awful but certainly makes much sense. One can perhaps picture the scene as the servants began to add more and more water to the wine they served. Perhaps many of the guests had consumed enough of the "good stuff" to make them a little "tipsy," thereby preventing them from fully appreciating what was being done to them. I am not a connoisseur of wine—never have been, but I am certain that watered down wine was an insult to the host and to the hostess. This did not reflect very well on their social standing. They weren't as concerned about having their nails done properly or wearing the right dress as many are today. Really, the hallmark of a marvelous wedding was the quality of the wine that was served at the table. And, so it was, they would eventually get to the point at which the guests were literally drinking nothing but colored water.

The scene was set. It was time for dramatic action. There was nothing more the father of the bride could do to avert a catastrophe! Then something dramatic happened.

On the third day a wedding took place at Cana in Galilee. Jesus' mother was there, and Jesus and His disciples had also been invited to the wedding. When the wine was gone, Jesus' mother said to Him, "They have no more wine." "Dear woman, why do you involve me?" Jesus replied. "My time has not yet come."

Although it may appear that Jesus was being rude to His mother this is not an arrogant statement. Jesus was not disrespecting his mother. He was not behaving in a macho way, or being ungentlemanly. Jesus knew that she knew He was capable of fixing this problem. Of all the people who would understand Mary would do so. She had pondered many things in her heart concerning this son she had brought into this world. She knew that this human predicament would present little problem to the Son of man. Perhaps we could put it like this:

"What concern of this is yours? You know better than that mom! You know that my hour has not yet come. You understand that the purpose for which I am in this place has nothing to do with this moment in time, but rather with the sacrifice I am willing to make, because I, the Son of Man, was willing to lay down and lay aside the privilege of being with God in

Heaven, and to take up the mantle of the sinfulness of man, even though I am without sin."

It should come as no surprise, then, that Jesus' mother readily instructed the servants to do whatever it was Jesus would tell them to do. Mary understood one of the most basic of all Christian principles. Just do whatever Jesus tells you to do.

By the way, Jesus had not said anything yet. She just knew. And so, we have this rather remarkable explanation.

> Nearby stood six stone water jars, the kind used by the Jews for ceremonial washing, each holding from twenty to thirty gallons. Jesus said to His servants, "Fill the jars with water"; so they filled them to the brim. Then He told them, "Now draw some out and take it to the master of the banquet."

Why draw them out? Because they couldn't walk around with thirty gallon pots of water, so they had smaller chalices to transport the water. They would literally dip these in and take them, and they would pour that water into the jars that had previously contained the wine. Now, watch what happens here in verse nine:

"When the Chief Servant tasted the water after it had become wine, he did not know where it came from, though the servants had drawn the water he knew. He called the groom and told him, 'Everybody sets out the fine wine first, then after the people have drunk freely, the inferior wine; but you have kept the fine wine until now.' Jesus performed this first sign in Cana of Galilee, and by so doing, displayed His glory, and His disciples believed in Him."

As you pray for your miracle consider this wonderful story. I am sure there are several other reasons why this took place but I want to focus briefly on the top four:

1. **To demonstrate God's power.** The first reason Jesus' miracles are given in the New Testament is as a public demonstration of the ability of God to do what only He can do. What power! If you take that element out of a miracle, you have every reason to question whether or not it is of God. A miracle is something that only God can do!

2. **To glorify God's name.** The second reason miracles happened in the New Testament was

to give glory to the name of God. This passage is pretty evident. One minute the wine was gone, the next they obeyed Him and the water became the finest wine they had ever tasted. Jesus displayed His glory and His disciples believed in Him.

3. **To illustrate man's dependence.** In the words of the hymn writer; "Without Him I can do nothing." Who is man and who am I? Miracles are designed to illustrate man's dependence on God. They had no more wine; there was nothing they could do! Jesus' mother knew they could depend on Him. Perhaps it was from personal experience, or perhaps she had pondered these things in her heart; but nevertheless she knew that only Jesus could solve this problem.

4. **To strengthen man's faith.** As parents we want to teach our children that they can trust us to take care of them. We do that by being faithful to meet their needs physically and emotionally. Every time we feed them, hold them, take care of them when they are sick, and listen to them when they need to talk, we are building trust. It is the same

with our heavenly Father. Every time God does something for me, I trust Him more. When He performs a miracle in my life, He strengthens my faith in Him. Every miracle recorded in the Bible resulted in a stronger faith on the part of those who witnessed it. God is faithful; therefore we can have faith in Him! The first miracle Jesus performed at the wedding in Cana strengthened His disciples' faith in Him.

Just like you, I love this wonderful narrative about Jesus' first miracle. It is no accident because everything Jesus did in His life and ministry was designed for the people He loves. Nothing happened to Him, through Him, or by Him that does not apply to you and me. This wedding was least of all about a wedding and most of all about an incredible miracle. Incredible, yes, unbelievable no! Miracles are incredible things. They are hard to imagine but simple to believe. The simplicity with which we believe in them is the simplicity with which all believers are called on to "walk by faith and not by sight." Faith means we simply trust in God's ability to do all He has promised to do for those who love Him. If you have given your life to Christ by faith it means you have placed your life in His hands and have trusted Him to do above and beyond all you could ask or even think. The miracle you may be looking for is not simply yours for the asking. God is not a simple text message away, even though we can "text" Him at any time with anything we need to tell Him about. Miracles are not just waiting in God's post office for you and me to come by and pick up at our own choosing. No, I believe what took place at Cana provides some key insights into all that the Lord can and will do for us according to His divine will and purpose.

Some of our questions can be answered by taking a closer look at the seven elements present in the miracle that Jesus performed at Cana of Galilee. These seven elements were not only present on this occasion, but they are functional elements of miracles to this day. God hasn't changed His mind. I am completely convinced today as I pray for people who are asking God for a miracle, that a miracle is something that only God can do. This thought is worth repeating over and over again! In my own ministry I am trying to remember this fact.

I love the privilege of being the pastor of a local congregation of people. Like most churches, we have numerous meetings to make decisions regarding the work of the church. Of course there are so many wonderful opportunities to serve the Lord and we do our best to recognize these opportunities. Many of them simply mean we need to "go to work" doing exactly what the Lord has put in our hearts. But we try to remind one another that the greatest work done for Christ is the work we are called to do that we cannot do but for the Lord. Surely the work of the Lord ought to be about doing the things that only God can do. Perhaps we have not raised the bar high enough?

A miracle is something that only God can do, and when He does it. WHEW! We see His glory! I think it's time that we start understanding the actions and the activities of a God who loves us despite ourselves. In our churches, out on the mission field, wherever we are, it seems to me, more and more in our day and age with emerging technology and gadgets, we've come to believe that as long as we're able to do what we think we can do, that God's engaged in what we're doing. Not according to the Word of God! It is time that we fall upon our faces and say, "Oh God, I don't know what else to do." And God says, "Okay, I'll give you a miracle."

I cannot emphasize to you enough that miracles are impossible things made possible by the power of God. Miracles are the show and tell of the power of God. Many of our churches today have forgotten what it means to ask God to do something for us that we cannot do for ourselves.

Most Sunday mornings our ministry team gathers for prayer long before most of our people start arriving for worship. Simply stated our collective prayer is, "Lord, we have prepared a message from God's Word, the choir has practiced for hours on end and the orchestra is ready. Lord, we have an order of worship, and we've done everything we know we ought to do. We are doing it to the best of our ability, but take it all Lord. It all belongs to You and You alone. What we want is a miracle to come down upon this place." And so it ought to be in our personal lives. Perhaps the Lord wants us to do all He tells us to do and then trust Him to do only what He can do. Such is the character of a true miracle.

It would seem to me that there are seven elements present in every miracle. They are presence, predicament, purpose, parameter, practice, power and possibility.

The Seven Elements

1. **Presence.** The Bible says Jesus was there in Cana at the wedding. This miracle would not have taken place without His presence. You take the Lord Jesus Christ out of the equation and you will have no miracle. Do you have Jesus living in you? Have you asked Jesus to come into your heart? Is Jesus with you? You must be sure of this, and you can be sure of this! Salvation is the greatest of all miracles. The fact that a Holy God would forgive your sins against Him and come to live in your heart and life is too amazing. Let alone living eternally with Him in Heaven! Now that's a miracle my friend! Perhaps you need to trust Him as your Lord and Savior right now. Pray this prayer from your heart: "Lord Jesus, I am a sinner. I repent of my sin. Please forgive me of my sins, and come into my heart. I trust in You by faith and receive You into my heart and life." Now remember that His presence is the essential element of any miracle. So, as you look for this miracle, talk to Him, ask

of Him, trust in Him and bless Him when He grants you what you ask for.

2. **Predicament.** The second element of a miracle is predicament. In reality this wedding predicament presented an insurmountable obstacle. The facts were on the table and there was no solution likely. Short of the Master of the ceremony simply calling all the guests together and breaking the bad news to them, nothing could be done to provide them with replenished drinks that tasted good. Their predicament was absolute. They had nowhere to go, nothing to give and no one to turn to. This is why salvation is the greatest miracle! Because Jesus Christ is the only One we can turn to. There is no other way. There are no others who can save us from our sin. The miracle of salvation delivers man from an absolute predicament by which he can never find peace with God except through the Lord Jesus Christ. In the same way, only Jesus' presence can provide the miracle you are praying for when you and I understand that only He can do it. Are you in such a predicament?

3. **Purpose.** The third element of a miracle is purpose. In verse four Jesus explained His purpose. This verse explains the deep things of God and the fundamental purpose for which Jesus Christ died, and why He wants us to be whole again.

4. **Parameter.** The fourth element of a miracle is parameter. Parameters are rules of engagement. Jesus' mother said, "Do whatever He tells you." These were the parameters—just do whatever He tells you. The call of God in my own life began with a clear set of parameters. Well over three decades ago my wife and I were in South Africa where we were born and raised. We were young and had just gotten married. God spoke to us and said, "Go to America." We had no money to even buy a ticket to get here. To complicate things even more, we owed the government money for school loans. There was no way the government would give us permission to move to America. We were in a predicament. We needed a miracle. My wife came to me and said, "We need to sell all of our belongings, wedding gifts included, so we can be obedient

to God." We sold everything we owned, had exactly enough to pay all of our loans to the government of South Africa, buy two tickets to America, with $1400 left in our pocket. Little did we know when we arrived in New York City that $1400 would hardly buy two Big Macs! But we survived. Little did we know that God would use us to teach for many years at the New Orleans Seminary, or that He would use us in such a wonderful ministry to the people at First Baptist Church, in Spartanburg, South Carolina. Little did we know that one day I would be the pastor to Dr. Billy Graham. Little did we know that God would allow me to write books and "share God's truth with a desperate world" through The Encouraging Word broadcast ministry. But God did! He set the rules for engagement and we did our level best to follow them in every way. Another example may involve the challenges many of our young people face today. While I am so grateful for the scores of parents who are really doing such a wonderful job setting parameters for their children and raising them so well, there are some who are "falling through the cracks" of our modern society. This has always been true in every generation. But the world is changing at such a rapid rate. And with this change has come an avalanche of new challenges for our kids. In today's world it is really hard to set parameters, let alone to know what parameters to set! We must pray for our teenagers! So, if you are praying for a miracle in the life of one of your children, just think about the fact that Jesus set an entire pattern for the servants to follow—in order for them to receive their miracle.

5. **Practice.** The fifth element of a miracle is practice. The servants went out and did exactly what Jesus told them to do. Are we willing to be obedient and do exactly what Jesus tells us to do? Once we know the parameters, are we willing to follow whatever he tells us? I was playing with my grandson, Bolt, recently and we had toys scattered all over the place. When it was time to clean up, I said, "Bolt, it's time to put all the toys away. Big Chief (that's my grandfather name) has to go and get on an airplane now." Bolt

picked up one toy, threw it into the toy box and said, "Did it!" I must admit it was really cute, but I had to explain to little Bolt that all the toys had to be put in the toy box. How many times does God give us the parameters and we do one thing He tells us to do, but we do not finish the job? We must do exactly what Jesus tells us to do.

6. **Power.** The sixth element of a miracle is power. In Verse 10, the power of God was demonstrated, and God in His infinite wisdom, and by His mighty power, through his Son, the Lord Jesus Christ, demonstrated that the best indeed can be served last. God's power cannot always be easily seen or defined. When Harry Kinard stepped into the room with Andrew for the first time God's power was there. As Christians we just know it. We feel it. The Holy Spirit reveals it! Perhaps we are not looking for His power? Perhaps we are not trusting in His power? God's power is the manifestation of Himself in ways we cannot necessarily describe. It is the demonstrated action of God who does what He does just because He is God! Often

we see God's power in the rear view mirror. And often we are privileged to bear witness to his power right then and there! On the spot, so to speak. Ask the Lord to open your spiritual eyes so that you can see his power. And, when you do see His power, thank Him first, and then tell everyone you possibly can tell. Bear witness to the power of God. In so doing, you may be bearing witness to an extraordinary act of God—a miracle!

7. **Possibilities.** The seventh element of a miracle pertains to the limitless potential and endless possibilities that God brings to bear on all who love Him. Herein lies the contagious effect of miracles. What the Lord does for you He intends to be used to glorify His name everywhere. This is what we read about in verse eleven of this great story—all the people were blessed. It's the contagious effect of a miracle of God. When God moves, the possibilities are endless. I know a lady who has spent the better part of her life living in sin. Sadly, she still just doesn't get it. She has repeatedly turned her back on the Lord. Her parents have almost given up.

She's now close to 50 years of age and has
gone through many "ups and downs." She
carries tremendous hurt and pain in her
heart, some with great cause. She has been
treated unjustly, has been abused, has been
neglected—and she has brought so much
on herself too. This lady has made many
poor choices in life, has been rebellious and
disobedient, has defied and decried authority
and has walked away from many gestures of
love and grace. Above all else, she has refused
to surrender to the Lordship of Christ who
demands our everything. Oh yes indeed. This
lady is incredibly gifted. She has so much
to offer the Lord. She has such a vibrant
personality. But the years are going by and
she simply will not surrender her life to the
Lordship of Christ. We are praying now for
a miracle. Only God can do what only God
can do. We believe it! And, what's more—we
believe that when He does—well, the best is
yet to be!

Seven Steps to a Miracle

I DON'T KNOW what kind of problems you may be dealing with, but I do know that the Lord has impressed on me some practical steps to take in this regard. To make them a little easier to follow I have labeled them "The Seven Steps in Praying for a Miracle". I know you will "tweak" them to suit your own need for a miracle without stepping outside of what God's Word teaches. I am trying to practice these steps in my life and I know what a tremendous blessing they have been to hundreds of other people as well. Ask God to speak to you as you read these steps. Get a sheet of paper and write them down. Put them in your Bible. Tape them on your mirror. Keep them in your car as you travel. Keep them before you as you pray for those things in your life. These are practical steps. You can use them in your church, your personal life, and to help other people. They include, identify what is going on, write it down, form partnerships, pray, follow instructions, anticipate, and respond.

The Seven Steps

1. **Identify what is going on.** The greatest problem most people have is that they refuse to identify the problem they're having. It is easy to sweep a problem under the carpet and pretend it does not exist. On the other hand, it is easy to think the problem is one thing, when it is really something all together different. Be honest with yourself and ask God to help you identify the real issue.

2. **Write it down.** Every time I meet with my staff and with our ministry team, I continually tell them to write down their idea or plan. If you can't write it, you don't know it. You know there are just thousands of people who have wonderful ideas, but until you write it down, it'll always just be an idea.

3. **Form partnerships.** Form partnerships with other Christians—purpose-driven partnerships! All of us know precious people who are God anointed, grace filled people who are prayer warriors and partners in the ministry to which we've been called. Go to those people. This is not a matter of just selecting someone. Pray about it and form a partnership with the person God lays on your heart. Perhaps this may be a Bible-study group you enjoy, or a prayer group. Share your issue with them and ask them to pray with you about it in a meaningful way. Open your heart to them and, if needed, ask them to keep your situation confidential. In fact, if your need for a miracle is very personal, then I would counsel you to only choose one person perhaps. It still amazes me how many confidential things are passed around churches in the name of "prayer requests."

4. **Pray.** Just do it. Often we talk about our prayer requests to our friends until we are blue in the face, and we never get around to talking to God! I've been married for over 30 years to the most beautiful girl in the

world. When I first met Karyn, I remember dating her, and that was the first time I really began to learn about prayer. In our very early dating months I even recall a rather humorous incident involving prayer. When the time came for me to drop my "girl" off at her dorm after one of our dates I felt the "urge" to kiss her like she had never been kissed before! All the other couples around us were! At the very moment of impact Karyn stopped me and said, "Why don't we have a word of prayer together?" I was shocked and devastated to the core!! I can hear you laughing but she really did this to me. I think I had just learned my first real lesson about prayer! Seriously, that was the beginning of God doing something incredible in my life. He did and continues to work miracles in my life to this day. We often talk about prayer, but I submit to you there is nothing more significant than getting down to business and having a conversation with our Heavenly Father. Pray! Just do it! Your Heavenly Father wants an intimate relationship with you. You can say things to God that you cannot say to anyone else. Matthew 6:6–15 gives us instructions on how to pray. Take a moment now to read these verses. Jesus tells us to go into our prayer closet, or private place, close the door, and have an intimate conversation with Him. You do not need to be concerned about what you say. Your Father knows what you need before you say it, but He does want you to ask. If you continue to read these verses you will see that Jesus talks about forgiveness. Jesus reiterates the idea of prayer and forgiveness in other places in the Bible as well. In Mark 11:25, Jesus says, "When you stand praying, if you hold anything against anyone, forgive him, so that your Father in heaven may forgive you your sins." Sin hinders our relationship with God. In order to pray for a miracle, we must have our lives in order with others and with God.

I received a phone call late one night from Dr. Billy Graham. He was at the Mayo Clinic and called to ask a question. Now folks, I do not believe he wanted an answer from me, I believe he wanted me to think. I have never been around a more humble or precious man. He talks to me about deep spiritual issues. His question to me was this, "Why did Paul pray and supplicate?" After much discussion we came to the conclusion that prayer is talking to God, but supplication is the attitude with which we speak to God. We must ask God for a miracle in an attitude in which we find ourselves coming into the presence of the King of kings and the Lord of lords. We have been given permission through the righteousness of God in Jesus Christ to come into holy presence. When I pray I am not calling the White House to ask a favor from the President of the United States. I'm not calling my local city councilman. I'm not merely going to my pastor. I am coming into the presence of Almighty God who is the Creator of the universe! God can do exceedingly abundantly above all that you and I ask or even think! Do you really believe that?

5. **Follow instructions.** Your prayer conversation with the Savior is a two way street. You talk to God, and He talks back to you. In the Lord's Prayer, Jesus said, "Thy will be done

on earth as it is in Heaven," but evidently as we try to understand what it means to have Heaven on earth, there are many of us who get on our faces and we ask God to do what only God can do, and when He tells us what to do, we don't do it. The truth is there are so many of us who just simply will not listen to God's instructions—let alone follow His instructions. I really believe that disobedience has become the scourge of the local New Testament church. This is a great struggle and challenge in my own life. I don't know how many times I have asked God to do something in my life—to do what only God can do, and I've been willing to identify it, to write it down, and to even form partnerships with gracious, godly men and women, and to seek God's face in prayer, but I have flat out refused to follow God's instructions. If your marriage is in trouble and you begin to go through the steps to receive a miracle, you will hear instructions from God that will be difficult to follow through on such as: "Take your wife on a date. Say you are sorry. Admit that you were wrong. Ask for forgiveness. Change your habits. Cut off ungodly relationships with the opposite sex. Get home on time." You will receive many instructions from God. But the question is, "Are you willing to follow instructions?" We must be obedient to God's instructions before we can witness His miracles!

6. **Anticipate.** What a great word! Many times in my life, I have asked God for something and then I am surprised when He gives it to me! You want God to do something in your life that only God can do? Anticipate! The great Methodist preacher, John Wesley coined that phrase that we've grown to love so much—"Attempt great things for God; expect great things from God." Somehow in our theological context, we've become so pharisaical, and we've become so insipid within our own little cocoons, in our own religiosity, and deep sense of spirituality, that we have lost what it means to anticipate and expect an outpouring from a God who loves us despite ourselves. Many preachers have lost that great expectation of believing that God's word will never return void, and when

we stand in God's pulpit Sunday by Sunday, we've lost that keen sense of anticipation that God is in the saving business, and that Jesus Christ died for us. Probably the best example of anticipation was Jesus' mother. She didn't know what Jesus was going to do, or how he was going to do it, but she believed that He would do it. The word, "anticipate," points to a rejuvenation of the heart and gives believers framework in which to formulate an expectancy that God is actually the God of miracles. The expectancy that God can do the impossible.

7. **Respond.** This final step is so important. At the very heart of the issue is gratitude. Remember the seven lepers Jesus told us about? God did a miracle in their lives and only one of them bothered to come back and say thank you. When God does a miracle in your life, how do you respond? Where's the testimony? A living testimony is still a vital component of God's means to connect with the people He loves. Have you noticed that there seems to be less and less of a demand and a mandate for people to stand up and

say "Jesus Christ has changed my life?" There's nothing more wonderful than the testimony of a changed life. If you are praying for a miracle I would strongly suggest you pre-determine the fact of your testimony. Make a commitment in heart and prayer that you will make known the wonderful hand of the living God in your life. Perhaps you may even tell your accountability partners of your intent and purpose to testify. It would be good for them to remind you of your promise. And, just try and imagine the numbers of people who will be greatly blessed by hearing about the way in which you prayed for a miracle—and God did it!

The Greatest Miracle

WE'VE TALKED ABOUT miracles all through this booklet, but actually I have saved the best until last. We often need a miracle or simply want a miracle. Everyone wants to be a part of something bigger than themselves. We often go through life and miss the greatest miracle of all. A miracle is something that only God can do! You may need the greatest miracle of all ... that is, the miracle of salvation! Only God can forgive our sin! Only God can save a sinner! Only God can redeem a person! Often we pray and pray and pray for a miracle, but if you have never accepted Jesus into your heart and experienced the greatest miracle of all, then all of your other prayers are futile. You can be sure of your salvation today! You can know that you know that you know you are saved and have experienced the greatest miracle of all. Once you accept Jesus into your heart, the Holy Spirit will come into your heart and life. He will guide you, convict you, and show you how to pray for the miracles you need in your life. If you have never accepted Jesus Christ as your Savior I would like to offer you this opportunity to act now. These three steps to experience the greatest miracle ever all come straight out of the Bible.

1. **Admit that you are a sinner.** The Bible teaches, "All have sinned, and come short of the glory of God." (Rom. 3:23) We must realize we are born with a sin nature and there is nothing we can do about it in our own strength.

2. **Believe in your heart that Jesus died on the cross for your sins.** This is a heart issue, not a brain issue. Believing in your heart is the key! Believe that Jesus is the only way to be forgiven of your sins. He is the perfect sacrifice before a holy God! (Eph. 2:8)

3. **Confess with your mouth that you are a sinner and that He is Lord of all.** Believing

in your heart in the first step, but you must confess it with your mouth as well. (Rom. 10:9)

4. **Repent from your sins.** Turn and walk in the opposite direction. When Christ comes into your life, you will be made a new creation. (Acts 3:19)

5. **Surrender your life to God.** When you pray and ask God to forgive you, He will put the Holy Spirit into your heart and life to work through you. When you give up and allow the Holy Spirit to work through you, you can conquer sin in your life. He will take away your sins and put His righteousness in you. (Matt. 16:24)

You can pray a prayer something like this:

Dear God, I know that I am a sinner. I know that I am separated from you by my sin. I know that on my own, I can do nothing to save myself. Only Jesus can save me. I believe in my heart that Jesus died on the cross for my sins. I accept what He did as a payment for my sins. I confess that you are Lord. I ask you to come into my heart and life today to save me. I give my entire life to you today. I surrender my life to you. I ask you to walk with me and guide me in my life. Lord, I ask you to speak to me and help me know how to live my life. I thank you for saving me today! In Jesus' name I pray. Amen

When you take the above steps, then God in His power performs the greatest miracle known to man. You will become as white as snow. Your sins will be forgiven. When God looks at you, He will only see Jesus and what He did on the cross for you. He will change you from the inside out! Then you can begin your new life in Christ. You can begin to pray for miracles in your life according to His will. The Holy Spirit will show you how to pray. You will begin to walk with Him, and He with you. You will know when to pray for a miracle and you will begin to recognize miracles in your life on a daily basis.

I pray that God will touch your heart and life today as you begin to pray for miracles in your life. God is good! He wants to give you miracles! He wants to bless your life. Be mindful to tell others about Him and his goodness as you live your life and experience His miracles!

Steps to Peace with God

1. God's Purpose: Peace and Life

God loves you and wants you to experience peace and life—abundant and eternal.

The Bible Says ...

"We have peace with God through our Lord Jesus Christ." *Romans 5:1, NKJV*

"For God so loved the world that He gave His only begotten Son, that whoever believes in Him should not perish but have everlasting life." *John 3:16, NKJV*

"I have come that they may have life, and that they may have it more abundantly." *John 10:10, NKJV*

Since God planned for us to have peace and the abundant life right now, why are most people not having this experience?

2. Our Problem: Separation From God

God created us in His own image to have an abundant life. He did not make us as robots to automatically love and obey Him, but gave us a will and a freedom of choice.

We chose to disobey God and go our own willful way. We still make this choice today. This results in separation from God.

The Bible Says ...

"For all have sinned and fall short of the glory of God." *Romans 3:23, NKJV*

"For the wages of sin is death, but the gift of God is eternal life in Christ Jesus our Lord." *Romans 6:23, NKJV*

Our choice results in separation from God.

People (Sinful)

God (Holy)

OUR ATTEMPTS

Through the ages, individuals have tried in many ways to bridge this gap ... without success ...

THE BIBLE SAYS ...

"There is a way that seems right to a man, but its end is the way of death."
Proverbs 14:12, NKJV

"But your iniquities have separated you from your God; and your sins have hidden His face from you, so that He will not hear."
Isaiah 59:2, NKJV

There is only one remedy for this problem of separation.

3. GOD'S REMEDY: THE CROSS

Jesus Christ is the only answer to this problem. He died on the cross and rose from the grave, paying the penalty for our sin and bridging the gap between God and people.

THE BIBLE SAYS ...

"For there is one God and one Mediator between God and men, the Man Christ Jesus."
1 Timothy 2:5, NKJV

"For Christ also suffered once for sins, the just for the unjust, that He might bring us to God."
1 Peter 3:18, NKJV

"But God shows his love for us in that while we were still sinners, Christ died for us." *Romans 5:8, ESV*

God has provided the only way ... we must make the choice ...

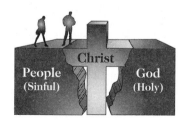

4. OUR RESPONSE: RECEIVE CHRIST

We must trust Jesus Christ and receive Him by personal invitation.

THE BIBLE SAYS ...

"Behold, I stand at the door and knock. If anyone hears My voice and opens the door, I will come in to him and dine with him, and he with Me." *Revelation 3:20, NKJV*

"But to all who did receive him, who believed in his name, he gave the right to become children of God."
John 1:12, ESV

"If you confess with your mouth that Jesus is Lord and believe in your heart that God raised him from the dead, you will be saved." *Romans 10:9, ESV*

Are you here ... or here?

People
Sin
Rebellion
Separation

Christ

God
Peace
Forgiveness
Abundant Life
Eternal Life

Is there any good reason why you cannot receive Jesus Christ right now?

HOW TO RECEIVE CHRIST:

1. Admit your need (say, "I am a sinner").
2. Be willing to turn from your sins (repent) and ask for God's forgiveness.
3. Believe that Jesus Christ died for you on the cross and rose from the grave.
4. Through prayer, invite Jesus Christ to come in and control your life through the Holy Spirit (receive Jesus as Lord and Savior).

WHAT TO PRAY:

Dear God,
    I know that I am a sinner. I want to turn from my sins, and I ask for Your forgiveness. I believe that Jesus Christ is Your Son. I believe He died for my sins and that You raised Him to life. I want Him to come into my heart and to take control of my life. I want to trust Jesus as my Savior and follow Him as my Lord from this day forward.
                        In Jesus' Name, amen.

_____   _____
Date   Signature

GOD'S ASSURANCE: HIS WORD

IF YOU PRAYED THIS PRAYER,

THE BIBLE SAYS ...

"For 'everyone who calls on the name of the Lord will be saved.'"
Romans 10:13, ESV

Did you sincerely ask Jesus Christ to come into your life?
Where is He right now? What has He given you?

"For by grace you have been saved through faith. And this is not your own doing; it is the gift of God, not a result of works, so that no one may boast." *Ephesians 2:8–9, ESV*

THE BIBLE SAYS ...

"He who has the Son has life; he who does not have the Son of God does not have life. These things I have written to you who believe in the name of the Son of God, that you may know that you have eternal life, and that you may continue to believe in the name of the Son of God."
1 John 5:12–13, NKJV

Receiving Christ, we are born into God's family through the supernatural work of the Holy Spirit, who indwells every believer. This is called regeneration or the "new birth."

This is just the beginning of a wonderful new life in Christ. To deepen this relationship you should:

1. Read your Bible every day to know Christ better.
2. Talk to God in prayer every day.
3. Tell others about Christ.
4. Worship, fellowship, and serve with other Christians in a church where Christ is preached.
5. As Christ's representative in a needy world, demonstrate your new life by your love and concern for others.

God bless you as you do.

Franklin Graham

If you want further help in the decision you have made, write to:
Billy Graham Evangelistic Association
1 Billy Graham Parkway, Charlotte, NC 28201-0001

1-877-2GRAHAM (1-877-247-2426)
BillyGraham.org/commitment

Pronounce It

PERFECTLY
in FRENCH

SECOND EDITION

Christopher Kendris
B.S., M.S., Columbia University
M.A., Ph.D., Northwestern University
Diplômé, Faculté des Lettres.
Institut de Phonétique,
Université de Paris (en Sorbonne)

Former Chairman
Department of Foreign Languages
Farmingdale High School
Farmingdale, New York

Theodore Kendris
Ph.D., Université Laval
Penn State University
Hazleton Campus
Hazleton, Pennsylvania

BARRON'S EDUCATIONAL SERIES, INC.

To St. Sophia Greek Orthodox Church
of Albany, New York, our parish

and

Yolanda, Alex, Tina, Fran, Bryan, Daniel, Matthew, Andrew,
Madeleine Sophia, Joe, Sue, Justin, Athena, Tom, Donna,
Amanda, Laura, Thomas William, Richard, Alice, Katherine,
Elizabeth, Hilda, Rachelle, Gilda, Hannah, Myron, Vera, Eva,
Frank, Walter, Lara, Alex, Tom, Diana
with love

© Copyright 2005, 1994 by Barron's Educational Series, Inc.

All inquiries should be addressed to:
Barron's Educational Series, Inc.
250 Wireless Boulevard
Hauppauge, New York 11788
http://www.barronseduc.com

Full Package
ISBN-13: 978-0-7641-7773-6
ISBN-10: 0-7641-7773-7

Book Only
ISBN-13: 978-0-7641-2929-2
ISBN-10: 0-7641-2929-5

Library of Congress Catalog Card No. 2004063839

Library of Congress Cataloging-in-Publication Data
Kendris, Christopher.
   Pronounce it perfectly in French / by Christopher Kendris and
Theodore Kendris.—2. ed.
      p. cm.
   Includes index.
   ISBN 0-7641-2929-5 (book)
   ISBN 0-7172-7773-7 (book/3 CDs)
      1. French language—Pronunciation by foreign speakers.
2. French language—Textbooks for foreign speakers—English.
I. Kendris, Theodore. II. Title.

PC 2137.K46 2005
448.3′421—dc22

                                                      2004063839

PRINTED IN CHINA
9 8

CONTENTS

Track List

CD 1
Track:

CD 2
Track:

CD 3
Track:

Preface to the Second Edition

Welcome to the second edition of *Pronounce It Perfectly in French*. A new major feature has been added: the use of the phonetic symbols of the International Phonetic Association (IPA) to help you improve your pronunciation of French.

We have also included a Guide to the Pronunciation of French Using the IPA Phonetic Symbols. After each phonetic symbol are examples of French words that represent a variety of spellings whose sounds connect with the phonetic symbols. Familiarize yourself with this special feature by following the guide carefully as you listen to the French speakers on the CDs. In this way, you can associate the phonetic symbols with the sounds of the French words you see in the guide and you hear on the CDs. We want to express our sincere appreciation to the staff of the SIL (Summer Institute of Linguistics) in Dallas, Texas, for providing us with the font for the IPA phonetic symbols, which we used while preparing this edition.

Another new feature of the second edition is Part Four, which offers extensive practice in context for your enrichment and, yes, even for your enjoyment. The new section contains a variety of selections that are also expressed in the IPA phonetic symbols, as well as in English translation. You can also hear the new selections in French on the CDs: for example, you can repeat during the pauses as you listen to popular phrases, famous lines of French poetry, proverbs, familiar sayings, selections from classical French literature (which are all in the public domain), tongue twisters, humor, and riddles.

It would be a good idea to become familiar with the table of contents so you can take advantage of all these useful features and many more. Enjoy!

C.K. and T.K.

Introduction

The lessons in this book and the CDs that come with it are organized and presented simply and clearly to help you improve your pronunciation of French. The program is appropriate for students in middle schools, high schools, colleges, universities, and adult education classes. You can use the program independently, in class, or in a language laboratory. Because of the wide variety of topics, travelers, businesspeople, those in government service or serving in the military, and others who want to learn to pronounce French properly will also find it useful. If you follow the book and CDs from beginning to end, spending at least one hour a day practicing, you will be amazed at the improvement in your French pronunciation.

The French language has musical qualities when spoken properly because of the abundant use of pure vowels, semivowels, and nasal vowels pronounced in a variety of ways. The language is never spoken in a monotone because it lends itself naturally to rhythm, intonation (a rise and fall of the voice), liaisons, *enchaînements* (linking, which is not the same thing as a liaison), elision, and other qualities. If you listen carefully to the authentic French spoken on the CDs, and if you let yourself go, doing your best to imitate the pronunciation on the tapes, you will be happy with the results.

We recommend you start at the beginning of the book with the basics and not jump around (unless it's for review or reinforcement) because the program progresses gradually from simple sounds to the more challenging ones. There is also constant review of sounds, weaving in and out, and back and forth. The book begins with the pronunciation of the letters of the French alphabet. You must be acquainted with them so you can see how their sounds change when used in different words. Also, it will be helpful when you hear the speakers on the CDs refer to a particular letter of the alphabet when the word is spelled for you. Part One introduces the vowels. You will learn how to pronounce them when they have no accent marks in different positions within a word, and how they change in pronunciation when they do have accent marks.

The lessons in this book are arranged systematically from the most simple and basic sounds of vowels and consonants to the most common single, double, and triple vowels in combinations, groups, and clusters with or without consonants within a word or at the end of a word.

Eventually, you are guided in the pronunciation of words in groups, phrases, clauses, sentences, and paragraphs. At that point, you are actively engaged in *real practice in context*. Review the table of contents and fan the pages of the book to see for yourself that the CDs give you plenty of practice in listening and speaking.

When we give English words as examples that contain sounds similar to French, remember that they are only approximate because the English language does not contain several of the French sounds. For example, when pronouncing a round, closed **o** in French, it should not contain a *w* sound tacked on to it as we do in English. When an English-speaking person says, for example, *Oh, so go!* the tendency is to tack on the sound of *w* after each of those three vowel **o** sounds. After all, the English words *so* and *sew* both have the same pronunciation! In French, you must avoid such an added *w* sound by not bringing your lips together.

Drawings are included in the book to illustrate the proper position of the lips and tongue and help you produce the sounds as accurately as possible.

French pronunciation varies in the regions of France and in other French-speaking countries and regions just as English is pronounced differently in the United States, Canada, Great Britain, Australia, and other parts of the world. Different levels of pronunciation can be heard in France within regions: for example, there is *la langue populaire*, literally popular language, often pronounced somewhat carelessly as we sometimes pronounce English incorrectly. For example, many English-speaking people pronounce library as *libary*, nuclear as *nucular*, escape as *exscape*, and many others, which you must have noticed.

La langue soignée is careful, literally well-groomed, acceptable pronunciation. The pronunciation of French recommended in this book and on the CDs is correct, *soignée*, and acceptable French that anybody in any level of society in French-speaking areas can easily understand.

Homophones are words that are spelled in different ways and have different meanings, but with the same pronunciation. These homophones are much more common in French than in English. Here is a typical example in French: *Le ver vert va vers le verre vert* ("The green worm is going toward the green glass"). That statement is a practice drill on the sound [vɛːr]. The mark ː indicates that the vowel sound in front of it is long—in other words, drag it out a little bit. Note the words, the spellings, the different meanings, and the same pronunciation for all of these homophones:

ver	[vɛːr]	*worm*
vert	[vɛːr]	*green*
vers	[vɛːr]	*toward*
verre	[vɛːr]	*glass*

That well-known statement illustrates the importance of spelling, sound, pronunciation, and meaning. The French language is rich in such homophones and we will offer you some useful and entertaining sentences and rhymes so you can practice them in this book and on the CDs.

The best method, taught in the Institut de Phonétique of the Université de Paris (en Sorbonne), uses spelling as a starting point to achieve perfect or near-perfect pronunciation. The training the main author of this book received at the Institut de Phonétique under Monsieur Pierre Fouché is designed for French teachers. It teaches the student how to determine the pronunciation of French words when faced with different spellings. For example, in English the addition of the letter *e* to the word *at* results in *ate*, which causes the vowel *a* to be pronounced differently. A foreign speaker learning to pronounce English must know rules governing the changes in pronunciation and meaning involved, both to recognize and to produce the sounds. In the same way, the addition or deletion of a vowel or consonant to an existing word in French changes the spelling of the word, which, in turn, reflects a different pronunciation and meaning. The same is true when accent marks are added to French words.

Now let's try to pronounce it perfectly in French. And enjoy!

Christopher Kendris, Ph.D.
Theodore Kendris, Ph.D.

Guide to the Pronunciation of French Using the IPA Phonetic Symbols

Phonetic Symbols of Oral Vowels	Some Spelling Examples in French Words	Approximate Sounds in English Words	Comments, Hints, Observations
[a]	patte, papa, collage, Paris	something like the vowel sound in Tom	a antérieur (front of mouth)
[ɑ]	pâte, pas, âge, vase	ah! art, alms	a postérieur (back of mouth, drop jaw)

Note: Some dictionaries and reference books that give phonetic symbols for French sounds do not use this [ɑ] symbol to distinguish the sound from the [a] sound listed above it. We agree with those reference books that retain the distinction in pronunciation between words such as **tache** [taʃ] and **tâche** [tɑʃ]. In this book we use both different sounds in order to show the difference in both pronunciation and meaning.

[e]	jouer, j'ai, gai, café, thé	gay, say, ate	e fermé (closed e)
[ɛ]	elle, jouet, valet, tête, poète, mais, j'aime, merci	egg, met	e ouvert (open e)
[i]	ici, il, lire, lyre, île, Paris	see	
[ɔ]	donne, Paul, or, mort, mode	up, mud, done	o ouvert (open o); drop your jaw a bit
[o]	pôle, mot, eau, gauche, chevaux, repos	oh! open	o fermé (closed o)
[u]	fou, vous, roue, août, loup	to, too, food	keep your lips apart, thrust forward a bit

ix

[y]	tu, rue, mur, eu, elle eut, du, su, sur, sûr	(not an English sound, but close to the sound of few without pronouncing the y sound that comes before the u sound or the w that comes after it)	see page 9
[ø]	feu, noeud, ceux, queue, peu	(not an English sound, but close to pudding)	thrust your lips forward a bit
[œ]	jeune, neuf, boeuf, peuple, peur	(not an English sound, but close to purr)	drop your jaw a bit
[ə]	je, me, premier, again de		this phonetic [ə] symbol is called e muet (mute e).

Phonetic Symbols of Nasal Vowels

[œ̃]	un, parfum	(not an English sound, but close to sung)
[ɔ̃]	bon	(not an English sound, but close to song)
[ɛ̃]	vin	(not an English sound, but close to sang)
[ɑ̃]	blanc	(not an English sound, but close to throng)

> **Note:** The four nasal vowels in the French language are all contained in this catchy phrase: **un bon vin blanc** (a good white wine).

Semivowels

[j]	yeux, dernier, lieu, mayonnaise	yes, yolk, yard
[ɥ]	lui, huit	(not an English sound, but close to "you + ee" without the y sound)
[w]	ouest, oui	west, wee

x

Phonetic Symbols of Consonant Sounds

[b]	bon, bébé	be, baby	
[d]	donne	done	
[f]	femme	fun	
[g]	gare, gai	gay, gum	
[k]	cou, café, cinq, quarante	can, kangaroo	*avoid* making an explosive aspirate *h* sound as in the English word *key*
[l]	bal, ballet	blame, long, tell	
[m]	madame	me, him	
[n]	banane	banana	
[ɲ]	signer, agneau	canyon, onion	
[ŋ]	le camping	camping, sleeping	
[p]	papa	pal	*avoid* making an explosive aspirate *h* sound as we do in the English word *puff*
[r]	Paris, rue	air, rude	

Some books that use phonetic symbols for French sounds sometimes use uppercase R instead of lowercase r. Remember that there is no equivalent in English. The French sound is pronounced farther back in the throat, at the uvula, the fleshy lobe you see hanging when you look in the mirror, open your mouth, and say aah.

[s]	silence	silence, pass
[t]	tutu	table
[v]	vent	village, live
[z]	zéro	zero, easy, shows
[ʃ]	chaise, chose	shows

Note that **la chose** means *the thing*; **chose** sounds very much like the English word *shows* without that *w* sound. To express a *ch* sound, as in *church, itch,* the phonetic symbol [tʃ] is used, as if spelled *tch.*

[ʒ]	je, garage	leisure, pleasure

Note: If you study, practice, memorize, write, and pronounce aloud the IPA phonetic symbols, you will be an expert in reading French without even looking at the French words. When French words are transcribed into these phonetic symbols, they reproduce the French sounds—if pronounced properly—even if you cannot read the words written in French! Isn't that remarkable?

The mark ′ indicates that the stress falls on the syllable after it.

Note also that the mark : indicates that the vowel sound in front of it is long.

Abbreviations and Marks Used in This Book

adj.	adjective	p.	person
e.g.	*exempli gratia* (for example)	part.	participle
		pl.	plural
etc.	*et cetera* (and so forth)	pol.	polite
f.	feminine	pron.	pronoun
fam.	familiar	s.	singular
i.e.	*id est* (that is)	sub.	subject
imp.	imperfect	subj.	subjunctive
ind.	indicative	1st, 2nd, 3rd	first, second, third
m.	masculine		

The mark ´ indicates that the stress (raise your voice a bit) is on the following syllable.

The mark ː indicates that the vowel sound in front of it is long when pronounced.

The French Alphabet

Introducing the Sounds

Let's pronounce the letters of the French alphabet. It is important to know the letters and how to pronounce them. Someone may have to spell a word for you to write down or you may have to spell a word to someone in French, for example, when you give your name to a hotel clerk over the telephone to reserve a room.

The 26 letters are the same as in the English alphabet. When referring to a French letter, each is masculine; for example: **un s, un t** /*an s, a t.*

On the CD, listen to the first 13 letters, A to M, and repeat each one during the pauses.

Now listen to the remaining 13 letters, N to Z, and repeat each one during the pauses.

Now listen to the speaker pronounce the French words used to designate the letters W, Y, and Z. W is **double v.** Y is **i grec.** The word **grec** means Greek; in other words, the Y is called a Greek i. Z is **zed** (also spelled as **zède**), and the pronunciation [zɛd] is the same either way.

Listen to this section on your CD again and repeat as many times as you need in order to master the sounds of the letters of the French alphabet.

Let's begin with Part One: The Vowels. In this part of the book and CD you will become familiar with the IPA phonetic symbols of oral vowels using many French words as examples. You will also receive instruction about how to pronounce vowels with or without accent marks, as well as the most common single, double, and triple vowels that come in combinations and clusters at the beginning, middle, or end of a word. You will also learn about the three semivowels and the four nasal vowels.

PART ONE
The Vowels

LESSON ONE
Thе Vowеls a, е, i, o, u

Introducing the Sounds

The letters of the French alphabet that represent vowel sounds are **a, e, i, o, u.** The letter **y** is a semivowel when it is pronounced like the vowel **i,** as in the French word *bicyclette* [bisi ˈklɛt] / bicycle. In the Middle Ages and the sixteenth century, **ami** and **amie** (friend) were written as **amy** and **amye.** In medieval manuscripts **y** was often used instead of **i** to avoid confusion if the **i** was written next to **n, m,** or **u.** In fact, **y** was often used at the end of a word, after a vowel. So in early printed books, in the 1500s, you'll find the word for *king* spelled **roy.** (Did you know that the name *Leroy* means "the king"?) At other times, the letter **y** is a semiconsonant, known as a *yod* [jɔd] sound, as in the English words *yes* and *yard,* and in the French word *mayonnaise* [majɔˈnɛːz]. If you find it difficult deciphering the sounds of the IPA phonetic symbols enclosed in [ ] for the French words, please review the Guide to the Pronunciation of French at the beginning of the book. Also, see farther on under the heading **The Semivowel *y*.**

The Vowel *a*

The French vowel sound **a** is pronounced in two ways. Sometimes it has the sound of the phonetic symbol [la], as in the word **la,** which is pronounced in the front of the mouth. The tip of the tongue touches the lower front teeth. The mouth is open. (See Figure 1.)

Remember that you pass the sound through your nose to say a nasal vowel. For an oral vowel you do not.

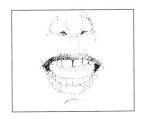

Figure 1.
The oral vowel **a**.

Now listen carefully to all the examples, repeat the French words after the speaker, then listen for the confirmation.

EXAMPLES

l**a**	[la]	*the, her, it* (f.s.)
m**a**	[ma]	*my* (f.s.)
s**a**	[sa]	*his, her, its* (f.s.)
t**a**	[ta]	*your* (f. 2nd p.s.)

[ɑ]

At other times the French oral sound of the letter **a** has the broad and wide sound of the phonetic symbol [ɑ], as in the words **âge** [ɑːʒ] and **coup de grâce** [kudgrɑːs]. Examples of that sound in English words are *ah! art, alms.*

EXAMPLES

pas	[pɑ]	***pas moi**/not me*
(le) **vase**	[vɑːz]	*vase*
(la) **vase**	[vɑːz]	*mud*
(le) **bas**-relief	[bɑrə´ljɛf]	*bas-relief, low relief*
(le) **passe**port	[pɑspɔːr]	*passport*
(l') **âge**	[ɑːʒ]	*age*
(la) **taille**	[tɑːj]	*size, waistline*

The mark ´ indicates that the stress (raise your voice a bit) is on the following syllable.

The mark : indicates that the vowel sound in front of it is long when pronounced.

The Vowel e

The French letter **e** is pronounced in different ways according to its position in a word. Let's start with the mute **e** sound (in French called **e muet** [ə mɥɛ]), which is expressed by the phonetic symbol [ə] . The closest sound in an English word for the correct pronunciation of [ə] is the first **a** in ag**a**in. Keep consulting the guide to the IPA phonetic symbols. After repeated use, you will find it easy and enjoyable when you recognize the phonetic symbols and can read them fluently. This bit of new knowledge adds to your educational advancement and your personal répertoire [repεr´twaːr]. It will also help you become aware of the correct pronunciation of difficult French words.

[ə]

EXAMPLES

le	[lə]	*the, him, it* (m.s.)
me	[mə]	*me, to me, myself*
se	[sə]	*himself, herself, oneself, themselves*
te	[tə]	*you, to you, yourself* (2nd p.s.)

Another sound of the vowel **e** is known as closed **e** (**e fermé**). It is expressed by the phonetic symbol [e]. This sound can have different spellings; sometimes there are vowel combinations that do not contain the vowel **e**. In English sounds, the closest is in the pronunciation of the sound in the spelling **ay,** as in p**ay,** s**ay,** d**ay,** and also in the English words p**ai**n, **a**t**e**, **eigh**t, sl**eigh.** Did you notice that these words have the same vowel sound in them but the sound is spelled in different ways? In French, as you have just seen, the same sound can be produced by different spellings. Note them in the following examples and at the indexes at the back of the book.

[e]

EXAMPLES

jou**er**	[ʒwe]	*to play*
parl**er**	[par′le]	*to talk, to speak*
(le) roch**er**	[rɔ′ʃe]	*rock*
(le) caf**é**	[ka′fe]	*coffee, café*
(le) d**é**	[de]	*thimble*
j'**ai**	[ʒe]	*I have*
g**ai**	[ge]	*cheerful*
m**es, tes,** etc.	[me, te]	*my, your,* etc. (possessive, pl.)

In addition to the different sounds produced by the oral vowel **e** [ə] and [e], there is a third commonly used sound known as the open **e** (**e ouvert**). That sound is represented by the IPA phonetic symbol [ɛ]. Here again, in French, different spellings produce that sound. In English sounds, the closest to the sound of [ɛ] is in the pronunciation of **e** in **e**gg, m**e**t, g**e**t. Note the French examples here and in the indexes at the back of the book.

[ɛ]

EXAMPLES

elle	[ɛl]	*she*
(le) jou**et**	[ʒwɛ]	*toy*
(le) val**et**	[va′lɛ]	*valet*
(la) t**ê**te	[tɛ:t]	*head*
(le) po**è**me	[pɔ′ɛm]	*poem*
m**ai** (m.)	[mɛ]	*May* (month)
m**ais**	[mɛ]	*but*
j'**ai**me	[ʒɛm]	*I like* (**aimer**)

The mark **:** indicates that the vowel sound in front of it is long when pronounced.

The Vowel *i*

The French oral vowel **i** is pronounced like *ee* in the English word *see*. The lips and tongue must be in proper position. Stretch the lips from side to side. The upper and lower front teeth are not touching but are very close to each other. Press the tip of the tongue hard against the lower front teeth. The back of the tongue does not touch the roof of the mouth. (See Figures 2 and 3.)

[i]

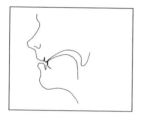

Figure 2. The oral vowel **i**. (side view)

Figure 3. The oral vowel **i**. (front view)

EXAMPLES

ici	[iˈsi]	*here*
(l') ami	[aˈmi]	*friend (m.s.)*
il	[il]	*he, it*
Miami	[miaˈmi]	*Miami*
(le) ski	[ski]	*ski, skiing*
(une) île	[yn il]	*isle, island*
y	[i]	**y** used as an adverb, (meaning *in it, there,* as in **allez-y**, go there, go to it)
Yves	[iv]	*Yves, Ives (man's first name)*
Vichy	[viˈʃi]	*Vichy,* name of a city in France

The mark ˊ indicates that the stress (raise your voice a bit) is on the following syllable.

In the following sentence the oral vowel **i** is used six times:

Mimi a mis ses amis à Miami.
Mimi dropped off her friends in Miami.

The Vowel **o**

The French oral vowel **o** is sometimes pronounced like the *o* in the English word *rose*. Do not bring your lips together when you pronounce **o** because you will produce a slight *w* sound, which is not desirable.

[o]

EXAMPLES

(la) r**o**se	[ro:z]	*rose* [Pronounce s as **z**.]
(le) p**o**t	[po]	*pot, jug* [Do not pronounce the **t**.]
all**ô**	[a´lo]	*hello* (when answering the telephone)
(la) vidé**o**	[vide´o]	*video*
P**au**le	[pol]	*Paula* (girl's first name)
(le) p**ô**le	[lə pol]	*pole*
(le) m**o**t	[lə mo]	*word*
l'**eau**	[lo]	*the water* (f. s.)
les **eau**x	[le´zo]	*the waters* (f., pl.)
g**au**che	[go:ʃ]	*left*
chev**au**x	[ʃə´vo]	*horses* (**le cheval, les chevaux**)
(le) rep**os**	[lə rə´po]	*rest, repose*
t**ô**t	[to]	*early*

The mark ´ indicates that the stress (raise your voice a bit) is on the following syllable.

The mark : indicates that the vowel sound in front of it is long when pronounced.

Note: In the boxes, notice all the different spelling combinations that produce the same sound. Aren't you glad you've learned the IPA phonetic symbols? Also, we hope you know by now that the mark ´ indicates that the stress is on the following syllable. The mark : indicates that the vowel sound in front of it is long.

And sometimes the French oral vowel **o** is pronounced something like the *u* in the English word *up* with the jaw slightly dropped.

[ɔ]

EXAMPLES

(l') **or**	[lɔːr]	*gold*
al**o**rs	[aˈlɔːr]	*then; so*
(le) p**o**rt	[lə pɔːr]	*port*
		[Do not pronounce the **t**.]
(la) p**o**rte	[la pɔrt]	*door*
		[Pronounce the **t**, but not the **e**.]
(je) d**o**nne	[ʒə dɔn]	*(I) give*
P**au**l	[pɔl]	*Paul (proper name)*
(la) r**o**be	[la rɔb]	*dress*

The Vowel *u*

Pronounce the French oral vowel **u** something like the sound of *u* in the English word *cute*. But be careful! When you pronounce the French **u,** do not bring your lips together because it will come out with a slight *w* sound as in the English word *you*. To produce the French **u** sound, form your lips as you would to pronounce the sound of **o**. With your lips in that position, pronounce the sound of the French **i** as in the English word *see*. The sounds of **i** and **o** were introduced earlier. (See Figure 4.)

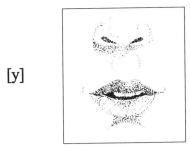

Figure 4.
The oral vowel **u**.

EXAMPLES

d**u**	[dy]	*of the, from the* (m.s.)
t**u**	[ty]	*you* (sub. 2nd p.s.)
s**u**	[sy]	*known* (**savoir**)
v**u**	[vy]	*seen* (**voir**)
n**u**	[ny]	*naked*
n**u**-pieds	[ny pje]	*barefoot*
(la) r**ue**	[la ry]	*street*
m**û**r	[myːr]	*ripe, mature*
j'ai **eu**	[ʒe y]	*I have had, I had, I did have* (**avoir**)
utile	[yˊtil]	*useful*
(la) l**u**tte	[la lyt]	*wrestling, struggle*
(la) l**u**ne	[la lyn]	*moon*
(la) b**û**che	[la byʃ]	*log*

The Semivowel *y*

The French letter **y** is pronounced like the French vowel *i* sound you learned earlier.

$$[i]$$

EXAMPLES

(le) cycle	[lə sikl]	*cycle*
(la) bicyclette	[la bisiˊklɛt]	*bicycle*
(le) cyclone	[lə siˊklɔːn]	*cyclone*

At times, the vowel **y** is also a **semivowel** or **semiconsonant.** It is sometimes pronounced as the *y* in the English word *yes*. In French, that sound is known as **le yod** (which happens to be the tenth letter of the Hebrew alphabet), as pronounced in the examples. In the word **pied,** for example, the vowel **i** followed by the vowel **e** produces the **yod** sound.

[j]

EXAMPLES

(le) **pied**	[lə pje]	*foot*
ayant	[ɛˊjɑ̃]	*having* **(avoir)**
(la) ma**y**onnaise	[la majɔˊnɛːz]	*mayonnaise*
il **y** a	[ilˊja]	*there is, there are* **(avoir)**
(le) **y**od	[lə jɔd]	*(French word for the y sound)*
les **y**eux	[leˊzjø]	*the eyes*
(le) l**i**eu	[lə ljø]	*place*
dern**i**er	[dɛrˊnje]	*last*
h**i**er	[jɛːr]	*yesterday*

The Vowels with Accent Marks

Introducing the Sounds à, â, é, è, ê, ë

The Accented Vowel à

[a]

The **accent grave** on the vowel **à** does not change the sound of **a.** It is pronounced exactly the same as **a** in **la, ma, sa, ta,** which you learned previously. The main reason why **à** *(at, to)* bears the accent mark is to distinguish its meaning, when written, from the verb form **a** *(has)*, which is the third-person singular present indicative of the verb **avoir** *(to have)*.

The **accent grave** is also used on the word **là** *(there)* to distinguish its meaning, when written, from the feminine singular definite article **la** *(the)*. They are both pronounced the same.

The **accent grave** is also used in the word **çà** in the adverbial expression **çà et là** *(here and there)* to distinguish its written meaning from **ça** *(that)*, which is a shortened form of the word **cela** *(that)*.

There is another French word that contains the **accent grave** on the vowel **a.** It is **déjà** *(already)*, as in the expression **déjà-vu** *(already seen)*.

These are the only four words in the French language where the **accent grave** is used on the vowel **a: à, çà, là,** and **déjà.** And, of course, on these compound words: **voilà** *(there you see)*, as in **voilà un taxi là-bas!** *(there's a taxi over there!)*; **holà** *(hey, there; stop!)*; **deçà et delà** *(here and there)*.

Now listen carefully to all the examples, repeat the French words after the speaker, then listen for the confirmation.

EXAMPLES

à	[a]	*at, to*
là	[la]	*there*
çà et là	[sa e la]	*here and there*
déjà	[deˊʒa]	*already*
déjà-vu	[deˊʒa vy]	*already seen*
voilà	[vwaˊla]	*there you see*
Voilà un taxi!	[vwaˊla œ̃ takˊsi]	*There's a taxi!*
là-bas	[laˊbɑ]	*over there*
holà	[cˊla]	*hey, there; stop!*
deçà et delà	[dəˊsa e dəˊla]	*here and there*

The Accented Vowel â

The **accent circonflexe** on the vowel **â** changes the sound of **a.** It is pronounced *ah,* toward the back of the mouth. The tip of the tongue touches the lower front teeth. The mouth is open a little wider than when pronouncing **à** or **la** above. (See Figure 5.)

[ɑ]

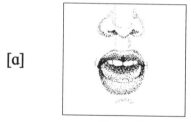

Figure 5.
The accented vowel **â.**

EXAMPLES

(l') âge	[lɑːʒ]	*age*
(le) château	[lə ʃaˊto]	*castle*
(le) câble	[lə kɑːbl]	*cable*

In some words the **accent circonflexe** is written over a vowel to indicate that, in the past, the letter **s** was written right after that vowel.

Examples

(la) h**â**te	[la ɑːt]	*haste*
(les) p**â**tes	[le pɑːt]	*pasta; pastes*

The Accented Vowel é

[e]

The **accent aigu** on the vowel **é** changes the sound of **e**. It is pronounced *ay*, as in the English word *day*. But be careful! When you pronounce *ay*, do not add that little *y* sound as in *yes*. The **é** sound is closed, clipped, and short. It is pronounced toward the front of the mouth. The upper and lower teeth are slightly apart. The tip of the tongue touches the lower front teeth. The lips are stretched a little, as if smiling. (See Figures 6 and 7.)

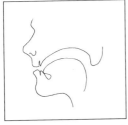

Figure 6. The accented vowel **é**. (side view)

Figure 7. The accented vowel **é**. (front view)

Examples

	d**é**jà-vu	[de´ʒa vy]	*already seen*
(le)	b**é**b**é**	[lə be´be]	*baby*
(le)	caf**é**	[lə ka´fe]	*coffee*
	all**é**	[a´le]	*gone* (**aller**)
	hât**é**	[ɑ´te]	*hastened, hurried* (**hâter**)
(le)	pât**é**	[lə pɑ´te]	*pâté*
	âg**é**	[ɑ´ʒe]	*aged*
(l')	**é**t**é**	[le´te]	*summer*

The Accented Vowel è

[ɛ]

The **accent grave** on the vowel **è** changes the sound of **e.** It is pronounced as in the English word *egg.* It is an open vowel sound pronounced toward the front of the mouth. The upper and lower teeth are slightly apart. The tip of the tongue lightly touches the lower front teeth. The lips are slightly stretched, as if smiling. (See Figures 8 and 9.)

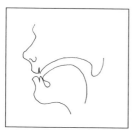

Figure 8. The accented vowel **è.** (side view)

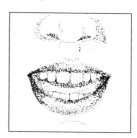

Figure 9. The accented vowel **è.** (front view)

EXAMPLES

(la) mère	[la mɛːr]	*mother*
(le) père	[lə pɛːr]	*father*
(le) frère	[lə frɛːr]	*brother*
très	[trɛ]	*very*
(la) flèche	[la flɛːʃ]	*arrow*
près	[prɛ]	*near*
(l') élève	[leˊlɛːv]	*pupil, student*

The Accented Vowel ê

[ɛ]

The **accent circonflexe** on the vowel **ê** changes the sound of **e.** It is pronounced as in the English word *egg,* the same pronunciation as **è** above.

EXAMPLES

prêt	[prɛ]	*ready* (m.s.)
prête	[prɛt]	*ready* (f.s.)
prêt-à-porter	[prɛtapɔrˊte]	*ready-to-wear clothing*
(la) dépêche	[la deˊpɛːʃ]	*dispatch*
Dépêchez-vous!	[depɛˊʃe vu]	*Hurry up!*
		(se dépêcher)
(la) bête	[la bɛːt]	*beast*
(la) fête	[la fɛːt]	*feast, holiday*
(la) tête	[la tɛːt]	*head*
(le) tête-à-tête	[tɛːt a tɛːt]	*private conversation between two persons*

In some words the **accent circonflexe** is written over a vowel to indicate that, in the past, the letter **s** was written right after that vowel.

EXAMPLES

(la) forêt	[la fɔˊrɛ]	*forest*
(les) vêpres	[le vɛːpr]	*vespers*

The Accented Vowel ë

[ɛ]

In some words, two dots called **le tréma** *(dieresis)* are placed on the vowel **ë** to show that it must be pronounced separately from the vowel in front of it. The **ë** is pronounced as in the English word *egg*. It is placed over the second of two adjacent vowels, creating two separate syllables, two separate pronunciations.

EXAMPLES

Citroën	[sitrɔˊɛn]	(name of a French automobile)
Noël	[nɔˊɛl]	*Christmas*
Israël	[israˊɛl]	*Israel*

Practice for Mastery

The speaker will now review the accented vowels introduced in Lesson Two.

Note: The examples used all appeared earlier in this lesson with their English translations. This time, however, they are not listed. Just listen and repeat each word or group of words after the speaker.

Now listen to the track again to review the words. This time, do the following exercises so you can fix in your mind the vowels with accent marks and the sounds they represent. With a pencil, complete the following words by writing the vowel and its accent mark. Pronounce the word aloud as you fill in each line. The answers are given in the box.

Exercise

1. ç___ et l___ ; déj___ -vu ; voil___ ; hol___
2. ___ge ; ch___teau ; h___te ; p___te
3. b___b___ ; caf___ ; all___ ; hât___ ; ___t___
4. m___re ; p___re ; fr___re ; tr___s ; él___ve
5. b___te ; f___te ; for___t ; pr___t
6. No___l ; Isra___l

Listen to the track again and check your answers before looking at the answers in the box.

Answers

1. çà et là; déjà-vu; voilà; holà
2. âge; château; hâte; pâte
3. bébé; café; allé; hâté; été
4. mère; père; frère; très; élève
5. bête; fête; forêt; prêt
6. Noël; Israël

Introducing the Sounds *î, ï, ô, û, ù*

Listen carefully to all the examples, repeat the French words after the speaker, then listen for the confirmation.

The Accented Vowel *î*

[i]

The **accent circonflexe** on the vowel **î** does not change the sound of **i**. It is pronounced exactly the same as **i** in **Mimi a mis ses amis à Miami** that you learned earlier under the vowel **i**.

EXAMPLES

fît	[fi]	(imp. subj., 3rd p. s. of **faire/** to do, to make)
(l') huître	[lɥitr]	*oyster*

The **accent circonflexe** is also used over a vowel to indicate that, in the past, the letter **s** was written right after that vowel.

EXAMPLES

(l') île	[lil]	*isle, island*
(l') îlot	[li′lo]	*islet, small island*

The Accented Vowel *ï*

[i]

In some words, two dots called **le tréma** *(dieresis)* are placed on the vowel **ï** to show that it must be pronounced separately from the vowel in front of it. The **ï** is pronounced *ee* as in the English word *see*. It is placed over the second of two adjacent vowels, creating two separate syllables, two separate pronunciations.

EXAMPLES

(l') héroïsme	[lerɔ´ism]	*heroism*
(le) maïs	[lə ma´is]	*corn*
Moïse	[mɔ´iːz]	*Moses*
mosaïque	[mɔza´ik]	*mosaic*
égoïste	[egɔ´ist]	*egoist*
naïf	[na´if]	*naïve* (m.s.)
naïve	[na´iv]	*naïve* (f.s.)

The Accented Vowel ô

[o]

When the **accent circonflexe** is placed on the vowel **ô,** it tells you to pronounce a well-rounded **ô,** like the *o* in the English word *over.* But be careful! When you pronounce English *o,* do not bring your lips together because you will produce a slight *w* sound, which is not desirable in French.

EXAMPLES

(le) diplôme	[lə di´ploːm]	*diploma*
(le) dôme	[lə doːm]	*dome*
(le) cône	[lə koːn]	*cone*
allô	[a´lo]	*hello* (when answering the telephone)

In some words, the **accent circonflexe** is written over the vowel to show that, in the past, the letter **s** was written right after that vowel.

EXAMPLES

(l') hôte	[loːt]	*host*
(l') hôtel	[lo´tɛl]	*hotel*
[Note that we have the word *hostel* in English, which is **une auberge** in French.]		
(l') hôtesse	[lo´tɛs]	*hostess*

The Accented Vowel **û**

The **accent circonflexe** on the vowel **û** does not change the sound of **u**. It is pronounced exactly the same as **u** in **du, tu, su,** which you learned earlier under the vowel **u**. It is used primarily to distinguish the meaning between two words that are spelled identically.

$$[y]$$

EXAMPLES

s**û**r	[syr]	*sure*
s**u**r	[syr]	*on*
d**û**	[dy]	*(past part. of **devoir**/should)*
		J'ai d**û** partir *(I had to leave)*
d**u**	[dy]	*of the, from the (m.s.)*

The Accented Vowel **ù**

There is only one French word that contains the **accent grave** on the vowel **u**. It is written as **ù** to distinguish its meaning, when written, from another word without that accent mark. Both words are pronounced like *oo* in the English word *too.*

EXAMPLES

o**ù**	[u]	*where*
o**u**	[u]	*or*

Practice for Mastery

The speaker will now review the remaining vowels with accent marks that concludes this lesson.

Note: The examples used are not listed here but may be found earlier in this lesson. Just listen and repeat each word after the speaker.

Now, skip back to the beginning of the track and replay the review of 15 words numbered 1 to 15. This time, with a pencil, circle what you hear in each of the numbered pairs. This is a quiz on sound differentiation.

Exercise

1. **la**	**lu**	6. **de**	**du**	11. **fit**	**fut**
2. **me**	**ma**	7. **hâte**	**hâté**	12. **île**	**îlot**
3. **sa**	**se**	8. **âgé**	**âge**	13. **héro**	**héroïsme**
4. **te**	**tu**	9. **le**	**lu**	14. **dôme**	**diplôme**
5. **port**	**porte**	10. **prêt**	**prête**	15. **dû**	**de**

Play the track again and check your answers before looking at the answers in the box.

Answers

1. lu	**6.** de	**11.** fit
2. me	**7.** hâté	**12.** îlot
3. sa	**8.** âge	**13.** héroïsme
4. te	**9.** le	**14.** dôme
5. port	**10.** prête	**15.** dû

*Accent*uate the positive! Listen to the pronunciation CD every day!

LESSON THREE

THE MOST COMMON SINGLE, DOUBLE, AND TRIPLE VOWELS IN COMBINATIONS AND CLUSTERS IN A WORD

Introducing the Sounds Featuring the Vowel *a*

Listen carefully to all the examples, repeat the French words after the speaker, then listen for the confirmation.

The Combination *ai*

Pronounce **ai** like *ay* in the English word *ray*.

$$[e]$$

EXAMPLES

j'**ai**	I have **(avoir)**
j'ir**ai**	I will go **(aller)**
je parler**ai**	I will talk **(parler)**

Note: In Lessons One and Two, the IPA phonetic symbols were used frequently to represent the sounds of the French words. This was done to help you learn them from the very start. Beginning with this lesson, the phonetic symbols are used when particular sounds are introduced to help you achieve the correct pronunciation. At times, the French words provided as examples of certain sounds are also given in phonetic symbols so you can continue reviewing them.

The Cluster *aient*

Pronounce **aient** like *e* in the English word *egg*.

$$[\varepsilon]$$

EXAMPLES

ils all**aient**	*they were going* **(aller)**
elles ir**aient**	*they would go* **(aller)**

Note, also, that **ai** in **balai** and **vrai** are also pronounced like **aient.** Same goes for **aid** and **ait,** as in **laid** and **lait.** They all sound like the letter *e* in the English word *egg*.

The Clusters *ail, aille, aillent*

Pronounce **a** as in the French word **la.** The vowel **i** before **l** or **ll** is pronounced like *y* as in the English word *yes*. But do not pronounce **e** or **ent.** They remain silent.

$$[a\!:\!j]$$

EXAMPLES

(le) trav**ail**	*work*
il/elle trav**aille**	*he/she works*
ils/elles trav**aillent**	*they work* **(travailler)**

The Cluster *aile*

Pronounce **ai** like *e* in the English word *egg*. Pronounce the **l,** but not the **e.** It sounds like the French word **elle.**

$$[\varepsilon l]$$

EXAMPLE

(l') **aile**	*wing*

The Clusters *aine* and *aîne*

Pronounce **aine** like *en* in the English word *ten*.

$$[\varepsilon n]$$

EXAMPLES

(le) capit**aine**	*captain*
(la) douz**aine**	*dozen*
cert**aine**	*certain*
afric**aine**	*African*
Jean de La Font**aine**	*(French poet)*
(la) ch**aîne**	*chain*

The Cluster *aire*

This cluster sounds like the English word *air*.

$$[\varepsilon \textrm{r}]$$

EXAMPLES

(l') annivers**aire**	*anniversary*
(le) dictionn**aire**	*dictionary*
ordin**aire**	*ordinary*
extraordin**aire**	*extraordinary*

The Combinations *ais, ait, aît, aix*

These combinations are all pronounced like *e* in the English word *egg*.

$$[\varepsilon]$$

EXAMPLES

m**ais**	*but*
franç**ais**	*French*

je v**ais**	I'm going **(aller)**
je parl**ais**	I was talking **(parler)**
je parler**ais**	I would talk
(le) l**ait**	milk
il parl**ait**	he was talking
elle parler**ait**	she would talk
il par**aît**	it seems **(paraître)**
s'il vous pl**aît**	please **(plaire)**
(la) p**aix**	peace

The **aix** in certain place names is pronounced like the English prefix *ex*, as in *ex-president*.

[ɛks]

EXAMPLES

Aix-*en-Provence*
Aix-*la-Chapelle*
Aix-*les-Bains*

The Cluster *amme*

Pronounce **a** as in the French word **la.** The **m** is pronounced but not the **e.** It sounds like the *om* in the English name *Tom*.

[am]

EXAMPLES

(le) gr**amme**	gram
(le) progr**amme**	program
(le) télégr**amme**	telegram

The Cluster *août*

Pronounce this cluster like *oo* in the English word *too*. It is also correct to pronounce the **t** so it sounds like *oot* in the English word *toot*.

[u]

EXAMPLE

août	*August*

The Combination *as*

Pronounce **a** but not **s.**

[ɑ]

EXAMPLES

tu **as**	*you have* **(avoir)**
(le) lil**as**	*lilac*
(l') embarr**as**	*embarrassment*
(le) p**as**	*step* (while walking)
p**as**	*not* (to negate a verb)
je ne sais p**as**	*I do not know* **(savoir)**
Edgar Deg**as**	(French artist)

Pronounce the **s** in the following words:

[ɑːs]

(l') **as**	ace	mar**s**	*March*
And in:			
Camille Saint-Saëns **[sɛ̃ sɑ̃ːs]**			
(French composer and organist)			

The Combinations *au, aud, aut, aux*

These combinations are all pronounced like *o* in the English word *over*. But be careful! When pronouncing the vowel *o*, do not bring your lips together because you will produce a *w* sound, which is not desirable in French.

[o]

EXAMPLES

au	*at the, to the* (m.s.)
(le) café **au** lait	*coffee with milk*
ch**aud**	*hot*
cost**aud**	*strong, robust man*
h**aut**	*high*
il f**aut**	*it is necessary* (**falloir**)
(l') artich**aut**	*artichoke*
aux	*at the, to the* (m./f., pl.)
(les) chev**aux**	*horses*
(les) journ**aux**	*newspapers*
Arthur Rimb**aud**	(French poet)
François Truff**aut**	(French film director)

Practice for Mastery

The speaker will now review all the combinations and clusters featuring the vowel **a**.

Note: These examples, which are not listed here, appeared earlier in this lesson. Just listen and repeat each word or group of words after the speaker.

Now go back to the beginning of the track and replay the review of eight words or groups of words numbered 1 to 8. This time, with a pencil, circle what you hear in each of the numbered pairs. This is a quiz on sound differentiation.

EXERCISE

1. **je**	**j'ai**
2. **maïs**	**mais**
3. **j'irai**	**j'irais**
4. **je parlerai**	**je parlerais**
5. **à**	**au**
6. **le cheval**	**les chevaux**
7. **les journaux**	**le journal**
8. **l'aile**	**le lait**

Go back to the beginning of the track and check your answers before looking at the answers in the box.

ANSWERS

1. j'ai	**4.** je parlerais	**7.** les journaux
2. mais	**5.** au	**8.** le lait
3. j'irai	**6.** les chevaux	

Practice in Context

Now listen to a short dialogue in which several combinations or clusters containing the vowel **a** are used. During the pauses, repeat each passage after the speaker.

Maman: Je vais au cinéma. Je rentrerai tard.

Papa: Et le travail que tu fais?

Maman: Je le finirai plus tard.

Papa: J'irais au cinéma aussi, mais je travaille dans la cuisine. J'ai le rosbif aux champignons et les ailes de poulet dans le four.

Maman: Oh, j'adore les ailes de poulet!

Papa: Je sais, je sais.

Maman: Amuse-toi dans la cuisine, chéri. À plus tard!

Mom: I'm going to the movies. I'll be back late.

Dad: And what about the work you're doing?

Mom: I'll finish it later.

Dad: I'd go to the movies too, but I'm working in the kitchen. I have roast beef with mushrooms and chicken wings in the oven.

Mom: Oh, I love chicken wings!

Dad: I know, I know.

Mom: Have fun in the kitchen, darling! See you later!

Introducing the Sounds Featuring the Vowel e (A)

Listen carefully to all the examples, repeat the French words after the speaker, then listen for the confirmation.

The Combinations *eau, eaux*

These two combinations are both pronounced like *o* in the English word *over*. But be careful! When pronouncing the vowel *o*, do not bring your lips together because you should avoid the *w* sound in French.

[o]

EXAMPLES

(l') **eau**	*water*
(le) bat**eau**	*boat*
(le) chap**eau**	*hat*
(le) gât**eau**	*cake*
(le) mart**eau**	*hammer*
(les) **eaux**	*waters*
(les) bat**eaux**	*boats*
(les) chap**eaux**	*hats*
(les) gât**eaux**	*cakes*
(les) mart**eaux**	*hammers*
Jean Coct**eau**	(French poet, artist, film director)

The Combination *ect*

Pronounce **e** like *e* in the English word *egg*. Pronounce **c** like **k** and pronounce the **t.**

[ɛkt]

EXAMPLES

corr**ect**	*correct*
dir**ect**	*direct*

incor**rect**	*incorrect*
indi**rect**	*indirect*
inf**ect**	*stinking, filthy*
intell**ect**	*intellect*
sél**ect**	*select*

Do not pronounce **ct** in these words:

[ε]

asp**ect**	*aspect*
resp**ect**	*respect*

The Combinations ée, ées

These two combinations are pronounced *ay* as in the English word *day*. But be careful! Do not pronounce the slight *y* sound when you pronounce *ay*. And do not pronounce the final **s.**

[e]

EXAMPLES

(la) dict**ée**	*dictation*
(la) f**ée**	*fairy*
(l') id**ée**	*idea*
(le) lyc**ée**	*high school*
(les) dict**ées**	*dictations*
(le) conte de f**ées**	*fairy tale*
(les) id**ées**	*ideas*
(les) lyc**ées**	*high schools*
Marie est all**ée** au cinéma.	*Mary went to the movies.*
Hélène **et** Janine sont all**ées** chez elles.	*Helen and Janine went home.* **(aller)**

The Combination *ei*

Pronounce **ei** like *e* in the English word *egg*.

$$[\varepsilon]$$

EXAMPLES

(la) n**ei**ge	*snow*
s**ei**ze	*sixteen*
(la) p**ei**ne	*trouble, sorrow*
pl**ei**ne	*full*
(la) v**ei**ne	*vein; luck*

The Clusters *eil, eils, eille, eilles*

Pronounce them all like *e* in the English word *egg* plus a slight *y* sound as in the English word *yes*. Do not pronounce the final **s.**

$$[\varepsilon{:}j]$$

EXAMPLES

(l') ort**eil**	*toe*
(le) rév**eil**	*awakening*
(le) sol**eil**	*sun*
par**eil**	*similar* (m.s.)
verm**eil**	*vermilion, bright red*
(les) ort**eils**	*toes*
(les) rév**eils**	*awakenings*
(les) sol**eils**	*suns*
par**eille**	*similar* (f.s.)
(l') ab**eille**	*bee*
(la) corb**eille**	*basket*
(l') or**eille**	*ear*
(la) bout**eille**	*bottle*
(les) ab**eilles**	*bees*

(les) corb**eilles**	*baskets*
(les) or**eilles**	*ears*
Mars**eille**	(French city and famous seaport on the Mediterranean Sea)
Pierre Corn**eille**	(French poetic dramatist)

The Clusters *elle, elles*

In these two clusters, pronounce the first **e** like *e* in the English word *bell* plus the *l* sound. Do not pronounce the final **s.**

$$[\varepsilon l]$$

EXAMPLES

elle	*she, her*
Elle va à Paris.	*She is going to Paris.* **(aller)**
(la) chap**elle**	*chapel*
cru**elle**	*cruel* (f.s.)
qu**elle**	*which, what* (f.s.)
ré**elle**	*real* (f.s.)
Elle est b**elle.**	*She is beautiful.* **(être)**
Elle m'app**elle.**	*She is calling me.* **(appeler)**
(les) chap**elles**	*chapels*
cru**elles**	*cruel* (f.pl.)
qu**elles**	*which, what* (f.pl.)
ré**elles**	*real* (f.pl.)

Practice for Mastery

The speaker will now review all the combinations and clusters featuring the vowel **e.**

Note: These examples, which are not listed below, appeared in this lesson. Just listen and repeat each word or group of words after the speaker.

Now go back to the beginning of the track and replay the review of six words or groups of words numbered 1 to 6. This time, with a pencil, circle what you hear in each of the numbered groups. This is a quiz on sound differentiation.

EXERCISE

1. **les eaux**	**l'eau**	**elles**
2. **le couteau**	**le gâteau**	**les bateaux**
3. **les orteils**	**l'orteil**	**les corbeilles**
4. **la peine**	**la veine**	**pleine**
5. **le marteau**	**les marteaux**	**le couteau**
6. **le lycée**	**les lycées**	**les eaux**

Play the track again and check your answers before looking at the answers in the box.

ANSWERS

1. l'eau	**3.** l'orteil	**5.** le marteau
2. le gâteau	**4.** pleine	**6.** le lycée

In the following words, if **ct** is pronounced, circle YES. If it is not, circle NO.

EXERCISE

1. **correct** YES NO	2. **respect** YES NO
3. **aspect** YES NO	4. **infect** YES NO

ANSWERS

1. YES	**2.** NO	**3.** NO	**4.** YES

Practice in Context

Now listen to a dialogue in which several combinations and clusters containing the vowel **e** are used. During the pauses, repeat each phrase or sentence after the speaker.

Madeleine: Bonjour, Anabelle!

Anabelle: Bonjour, Madeleine!

Madeleine: Où est la belle Giselle?

Anabelle: Elle est allée à la chapelle.

Madeleine: Et Mireille? Où est-elle?

Anabelle: Mireille est allée à Marseille.

Madeleine: Elle est à Marseille? Quelle veine!

Anabelle: Et nous? Où allons-nous?

Madeleine: Allons boire une bouteille d'eau et manger quelques gâteaux!

Madeleine: Hello, Anabelle!

Anabelle: Hello, Madeleine!

Madeleine: Where is the beautiful Giselle?

Anabelle: She went to chapel.

Madeleine: And Mireille? Where is she?

Anabelle: Mireille went to Marseille.

Madeleine: She's in Marseille? What luck!

Anabelle: And what about us? Where are we going?

Madeleine: Let's go drink a bottle of water and eat some cakes!

Introducing the Sounds Featuring the Vowel e (B)

Listen carefully to all the examples, repeat the French words after the speaker, then listen for the confirmation.

The Cluster *emme*

Pronounce the first **e** like *e* in the English word *egg* + **m** sound.

$$[\varepsilon m]$$

EXAMPLES

(le) dil**emme**	*dilemma*
(la) fl**emme**	*laziness*
(la) g**emme**	*gem*

But pronounce **emme** ~
name *Tom* in this word:

[au

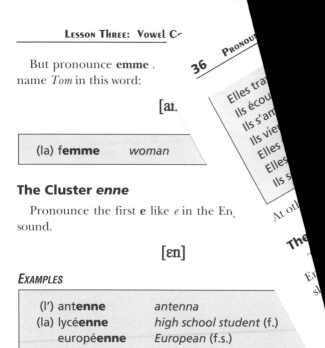

(la) f**emme**	*woman*

The Cluster *enne*

Pronounce the first **e** like *e* in the En~
sound.

[ɛn]

EXAMPLES

(l') ant**enne**	*antenna*
(la) lycé**enne**	*high school student* (f.)
europé**enne**	*European* (f.s.)

If the vowel **i** precedes **enne,** pronounce a slight *y* soun.
as in the English word *yes* plus the **enne** sound. This produces
the sound of the English word *yen.* Review the **yod** sound in
Lesson One.

[jɛn]

(la) chi**enne**	*female dog*
(la) chréti**enne**	*Christian woman*
(la) Parisi**enne**	*woman from Paris*

The Combination *ent*

When this combination is a verb form ending, do not
pronounce it.

EXAMPLES

Elles parl**ent.**	*They (f.) are talking.*
Elles écriv**ent.**	*They (f.) are writing.*

vaill**ent.**	*They (f.) are working.*
...t**ent.**	*They are listening.*
...us**ent.**	*They are having fun.*
...nn**ent.**	*They are coming.*
finiss**ent.**	*They (f.) are finishing.*
apprenn**ent.**	*They (f.) are learning.*
...e méfi**ent.**	*They mistrust.*

...er times **ent** is a nasal vowel. See Lesson Five.

Combination *er*

...he **er** infinitive form of a verb is pronounced like *ay* in the ...glish word *day*. But be careful! Do not pronounce the ...ght *y* sound when you pronounce *ay*.

[e]

Examples

all**er**	*to go*
parl**er**	*to talk, to speak*
donn**er**	*to give*
cherch**er**	*to look for, to search*

If the vowel **i** precedes **er,** pronounce a slight *y* sound as in the English word *yes* plus this **er** sound. Review the **yod** sound in Lesson One.

[je]

Examples

(le) prem**ier**	*first (m.s.)*
(le) dern**ier**	*last (m.s.)*
(le) pomp**ier**	*fireman*
(l') ac**ier**	*steel*
remerc**ier**	*to thank*
appréc**ier**	*to appreciate*

In many words that are not **er** infinitive endings, **er** at the end of a word sounds something like the English word *air*.

[ɛːr]

EXAMPLES

ch**er**	*dear; expensive* (m.s.)
(l') éth**er**	*ether*
(le) f**er**	*iron*
(le) chemin de f**er**	*railroad*
(l') enf**er**	*hell*
(le) scoot**er**	*scooter*
sup**er**	*super*

If the vowel **i** precedes **er,** pronounce a slight *y* sound as in the English word *yes* plus this **er** sound. Review the **yod** sound in Lesson One.

[jɛːr]

EXAMPLES

fi**er**	*proud* (m.s.)
hi**er**	*yesterday*
	[Do not pronounce the **h** in **hier.**]

When **er** is within a word, it is pronounced something like *er* in the English word *there*.

[ɛr]

EXAMPLES

m**er**ci	*thank you*
ét**er**nel	*eternal* (m.s.)
ét**er**nelle	*eternal* (f.s.)

(la) **fer**me	farm
(le) **ser**vice	service
je cher**che**	I am searching (**chercher**)

The Combination **ère**

This combination sounds like the English word *air*.

$$[\varepsilon\mathrm{r}]$$

EXAMPLES

(l') **ère**	era
ch**ère**	dear; expensive (f.s.)
(la) m**ère**	mother
(le) p**ère**	father
(le) fr**ère**	brother

If the vowel **i** precedes **ère,** pronounce a slight *y* sound as in the English word *yes* plus the **ère** sound, as you did in hi**er.** Review the **yod** sound in Lesson One.

$$[j\varepsilon\mathrm{r}]$$

EXAMPLES

fi**ère**	proud (f.s.)
(la) pri**ère**	prayer
(la) premi**ère**	first (f.s.)
(la) derni**ère**	last (f.s.)

The Cluster **erre**

Pronounce this cluster like the English word *air*.

$$[\varepsilon\mathrm{r}]$$

EXAMPLES

il **erre**	*he is roaming, wandering* **(errer)**
(la) t**erre**	*earth; land*
(la) gu**erre**	*war*

The Combination es

As a verb form, pronounce **es** like *e* in the English word *egg*. Do not pronounce the **s**.

$$[\varepsilon]$$

EXAMPLE

tu **es**	*you are* **(être)**

In the following words, pronounce **es** like *ay* in the English word *day*. But be careful! Do not pronounce the slight *y* sound when you pronounce *ay*. And do not pronounce the **s**.

$$[e]$$

d**es**	*of the, from the*
	(contraction of **de + les**)
l**es**	*the, them* (pl. of **le, la**)
m**es**	*my* (pl. of **mon, ma**)
s**es**	*his, her, its* (pl. of **son, sa**)
t**es**	*your* (pl. of **ton, ta**)

The Combination ès

This combination is pronounced like *e* in the English word *egg*. Do not pronounce the **s**.

$$[\varepsilon]$$

EXAMPLES

d**ès**	*from the moment when*
tr**ès**	*very*
(le) progr**ès**	*progress*
(l') exc**ès**	*excess*
(l') acc**ès**	*access*

Pronounce the **s** in **ès** here:

Licence **ès** Lettres	*Master of Arts degree*

[ɛs]

The **accent grave** is written on **ès** in the term **License ès Lettres** to distinguish it from the French verb form **es,** 2nd p.s., present tense of the verb **être**/*to be.* See **tu es** on page 39. Also, the **ès** in this term stands for **en les,** which means *in the;* in other words, the degree is a *Master of Arts in (the) Letters.* The **e** of **en** and the **s** of **les** combine to form **ès.**

In proper names, the **ès** is also pronounced like *ess* as in the English word *essay.*

[ɛs]

EXAMPLES

Pierre Mend**ès**-France	French political figure, president of the Conseil (1954–1955)
Sainte Agn**ès**	Saint Agnes

The Combination *ess*

Pronounce **ess** like the English word *ace* when it is at the beginning of a word.

[es]

(l') **ess**ai	*essay*
(l') **ess**ence	*essence, gasoline, petrol*
(l') **ess**uie-glace	*windshield wiper*
(l') **ess**uie-main	*hand towel* **(essuyer)**
essayer	*to try*

The Combinations *est, est-ce, c'est, est-ce que, qu'est-ce que*

In all these combinations, pronounce the verb form **est** like *e* in the English word *egg*.

$$[\varepsilon]$$

EXAMPLES

Ce fromage **est** frais.	*This cheese is fresh.*
Est-ce Louise?	*Is it Louise?* **(être)**
	[The **s** sound that you hear in **est-ce** is the **c** in **ce**.]
Oui, **c'est** Louise.	*Yes, it's Louise.* **(être)**

Also note these examples:

| **Est-ce que** Marie est malade? | *Is Mary sick?* |
| **Qu'est-ce que** tu fais? | *What are you doing?* **(être)** |

But when you pronounce **s** and **t** in **est** and in **ouest,** the words mean something else.

$$[\varepsilon st]$$

| (l') **est** | *east* |
| (l') ou**est** | *west* |

Practice for Mastery

The speaker will now continue to review additional combinations and clusters featuring the vowel **e.**

Note: These examples, which are not listed here, appeared earlier in this lesson. Just listen and repeat each word or group of words after the speaker.

Now go back to the beginning of the track and replay the review of ten words or groups of words numbered 1 to 10. This time, with a pencil, circle what you hear in each of the ten numbered pairs. This is a quiz on sound differentiation.

EXERCISE

1. **la gemme**	**la chienne**	6. **fer**	**fière**
2. **la flemme**	**la femme**	7. **est**	**est-ce**
3. **dernière**	**dernier**	8. **est-ce que**	**qu'est-ce que**
4. **tu as**	**tu es**	9. **chercher**	**je cherche**
5. **des**	**de**	10. **me**	**mes**

Play the track again and check your answers before looking at the answers in the box.

ANSWERS

1. la chienne	**5.** des	**9.** chercher
2. la femme	**6.** fer	**10.** mes
3. dernière	**7.** est-ce	
4. tu es	**8.** qu'est-ce que	

Practice in Context

Now listen to a dialogue in which several combinations and clusters containing the vowel **e** are used. During the pauses, repeat each phrase or sentence after the speaker.

La femme: Bonjour, Monsieur Bonnière.

Woman: Hello, Mr. Bonnière.

L'homme: Bonjour, Madame Detienne.

Man: Hello, Mrs. Detienne.

La femme: Est-ce que le chou est frais?

Woman: Is the cabbage fresh?

L'homme: Oui, madame, il est très frais.

Man: Yes, madam, it is very fresh.

La femme: Super! Est-il très cher?

Woman: Great! Is it very expensive?

L'homme: Non, pas très cher.

Man: No, not very expensive.

La femme: Avez-vous des choux de Bruxelles?

Woman: Have you any Brussels sprouts?

L'homme: Oui, madame.

Man: Yes, madam.

La femme: Est-ce que les pommes de terre sont très chères?

Woman: Are the potatoes very expensive?

L'homme: Non, madame, pas très chères.

Man: No, madam, not very expensive.

La femme: Oh, je ne sais pas. Mon père préfère les pommes de terre mais mon mari ne les aime pas. Ma mère préfère les choux. C'est un dilemme!

Woman: Oh, I don't know. My father prefers potatoes but my husband doesn't like them. My mother prefers cabbages. It's a dilemma!

L'homme: Et vous? Qu'est-ce que vous préférez?

Man: And you? What do you prefer?

La femme: Je préfère les asperges à la parisienne.

Woman: I prefer asparagus, Parisian style.

L'homme: Je n'en ai pas.

Man: I don't have any.

La femme: Alors, au revoir, monsieur.

Woman: Well, then, good-bye, sir.

Introducing the Sounds Featuring the Vowel e (C)

Listen carefully to all the examples, repeat the French words after the speaker, then listen for the confirmation.

The Combination *et*

When at the end of a word, pronounce **et** like *e* in the English word *egg*. Do not pronounce the **t**.

$$[\varepsilon]$$

EXAMPLES

(l') alphab**et**	*alphabet*
(le) ball**et**	*ballet*
(le) bonn**et**	*bonnet*
(le) carn**et**	*small notebook*
(le) paqu**et**	*packet*
(le) perroqu**et**	*parrot*
(le) poul**et**	*chicken*
(le) somm**et**	*top, summit*
(le) tick**et**	*ticket*
(le) gourm**et**	*connoisseur in the delicacies of the table*

The conjunction **et** is pronounced like *ay* in the English word *day*. Be careful! Do not pronounce the slight *y* sound when you pronounce *ay*.

$$[e]$$

et	*and*

The Cluster *ette*

Pronounce the first **e** like *e* in the English word *egg* plus the **t** sound.

[ɛt]

EXAMPLES

(la) devin**ette**	*riddle*
(l') étiqu**ette**	*etiquette; label*
(l') omel**ette**	*omelet*

The Combination *eu*

The word **eu,** meaning *had,* is the past participle of **avoir** *(to have),* as in **j'ai eu des nouvelles** *(I have had some news).* It is pronounced like the French vowel **u.** Review the sound of the vowel **u** in Lesson One. Also, the verb form **eut** is the third-person singular *passé simple* tense of **avoir.** The pronunciation of **eut** and **eu** is exactly the same.

But when at the end of a word, the combination **eu** is pronounced something like the *u* in the English word *pudding.*

[ø]

EXAMPLES

p**eu**	*little* (in quantity)
(le) f**eu**	*fire*
(le) j**eu**	*game*
(l') av**eu**	*avowal, confession*
bl**eu**	*blue*
(le) nev**eu**	*nephew*

When the vowel combination **eu** at the end of a word is followed by a consonant that is *not* pronounced, the sound of **eu** is the same as in the preceding list of words.

[ø]

EXAMPLES

je p**eux**	*I can* (**pouvoir**)
(les) f**eux**	*fires*
(les) j**eux**	*games*
(les) chev**eux**	*hair*
d**eux**	*two*
(les) bl**eus**	*blues*
il p**eut**	*he can* (**pouvoir**)
il pl**eut**	*it's raining* (**pleuvoir**)

When the vowel combination **eu** at the end of a word is followed by the consonant **s** plus **e,** which *is* pronounced, the
sound of **eu** is the same as in the preceding list of words. Note
that the **s** has a **z** sound.

[ø:z]

EXAMPLES

crém**eu**se	*creamy*
cr**eu**se	*hollow*
hid**eu**se	*hideous*
nerv**eu**se	*nervous*

When the vowel combination **eu** is followed by a consonant
that is pronounced *other than* the **s** or **z** sound, pronounce **eu**
something like *u* in the English word *curl.*

[œ]

EXAMPLES

œːr	
l**eu**r	*their; to them*
(la) fl**eu**r	*flower*
(le) bonh**eu**r	*happiness*
(la) p**eu**r	*fear*
(l') ordinat**eur**	*computer*

(l') h**eu**re	*hour*
le bébé pl**eu**re	*the baby is crying*

œf

n**eu**f	*nine*
(le) v**eu**f	*widower*

œːv

(la) v**eu**ve	*widow*
(le) fl**eu**ve	*river*
qu'il pl**eu**ve	*let it rain* (**pleuvoir**)
ils p**eu**vent	*they can* (**pouvoir**)
Catherine Den**eu**ve	*(French actress)*
(l') épr**eu**ve	*test*

œl

s**eu**l	*alone* (m.s.)
s**eu**le	*alone* (f.s.)
s**eu**ls	*alone* (m.pl.)
s**eu**les	*alone* (f.pl.)
(la) gu**eu**le	*mouth* (of an animal)

œgl

av**eu**gle	*blind*

œbl

(les) m**eu**bles	*furniture*

The Clusters *euil, euils, euille, euilles*

These four clusters are all pronounced the same. Pronounce **eu** as in **heure,** given above, plus the *y* sound as in the English word *yes.*

$$[\text{œːj}]$$

EXAMPLES

(l') écur**euil**	*squirrel*
(le) d**euil**	*mourning, sorrow*
(le) faut**euil**	*armchair*

(le) s**euil**	*doorstep, threshold*
(les) écur**euils**	*squirrels*
(les) faut**euils**	*armchairs*
(la) f**euille**	*leaf*
(le) portef**euille**	*wallet*
(les) f**euilles**	*leaves*
(les) portef**euilles**	*wallets*

The Combination *ez*

This combination is pronounced like *ay* as in the English word *day*. Be careful! Do not pronounce the slight *y* sound when you pronounce *ay*.

[e]

EXAMPLES

(le) n**ez**	*nose*
(les) n**ez**	*noses*
ch**ez**	*at the place* (home) *of*
ch**ez** nous	*at our place*
ch**ez** le docteur	*at the doctor's office*
vous av**ez**	*you have* (**avoir**)
vous all**ez**	*you are going* (**aller**)
vous parl**ez**	*you talk* (speak) (**parler**)
vous prononc**ez**	*you pronounce* (**prononcer**)

Practice for Mastery

The speaker will now continue to review additional combinations and clusters featuring the vowel **e.** This is the conclusion of that section.

Note: These examples, which are not listed here, appeared earlier in this lesson. Just listen and repeat each word or group of words after the speaker.

Now, go back to the beginning of this track and replay the review of 12 words or pairs of words numbered 1 to 12. This time, with a pencil, circle what you hear in each of the numbered pairs. This is a quiz on sound differentiation.

EXERCISE

1. **et**	à		7. **blé**	bleu
2. **sommeil**	sommet		8. **deux**	des
3. **nerveux**	nerveuse		9. **su**	ceux
4. **chevaux**	cheveux		10. **neveu**	neuve
5. **feuille**	feux		11. **j'ai**	jeu
6. **veuf**	veuve		12. **peu**	pu

Go back and check your answers before looking at the answers in the box.

ANSWERS

1. et	**7.** bleu
2. sommet	**8.** deux
3. nerveuse	**9.** ceux
4. cheveux	**10.** neuve
5. feuille	**11.** j'ai
6. veuf	**12.** peu

Practice in Context

Now listen to a monologue in which several combinations and clusters containing the vowel **e** are used. During the pauses, repeat each sentence or phrase after the speaker.

Je peux réciter l'alphabet comme le perroquet de Madame Claudette.

I can recite the alphabet like Mrs. Claudette's parrot.

Le perroquet s'appelle Asperge.

The parrot's name is Asparagus.

Il est bleu, jaune, et vert.

He is blue, yellow, and green.

Il a le nez grand.

He has a big nose.

Madame Claudette a le nez petit.

Mrs. Claudette has a small nose.

Elle est très vieille.

She is very old.

Elle est veuve, vous savez.

She is a widow, you know.

Elle parle peu.	*She talks little.*
Elle est toujours seule chez elle avec Asperge.	*She is always alone at home with Asparagus.*
Il est heureux et elle est heureuse.	*He is happy and she is happy.*

Introducing the Sounds Featuring the Vowel *i*

Listen carefully to all the examples, repeat the French words or phrases after the speaker, then listen for the confirmation.

The Combinations *id, ie, ies, is, it, ix, iz*

These are all pronounced *ee* as in the English word *see*.

[i]

EXAMPLES

(le) n**id**	nest
(la) dynast**ie**	dynasty
(la) géograph**ie**	geography
(la) papeter**ie**	stationery shop
(la) pâtisser**ie**	pastry; pastry shop
(la) v**ie**	life
(les) boucher**ies**	butcher shops
(les) pâtisser**ies**	pastries; pastry shops
(les) boulanger**ies**	bakery shops
gr**is**	gray
(l') av**is**	opinion; notice
(la) sour**is**	mouse
je d**is**	I say, I am saying (**dire**)
je l**is**	I read, I am reading (**lire**)
[But pronounce the **s** in this word: (le) l**is** *lily*]	

Par**is**	*Paris*
je su**is**	*I am* **(être)**
il écr**it**	*he writes, he is writing* **(écrire)**
elle l**it**	*she reads, she is reading* **(lire)**
(le) l**it**	*bed*
elle d**it**	*she says, she is saying* **(dire)**
(le) perdr**ix**	*partridge*
(le) pr**ix**	*price; prize*
(le) r**iz**	*rice*

But pronounce the **x** like **s** in these two words:

$$\begin{bmatrix} \text{sis} \\ \text{dis} \end{bmatrix}$$

s**ix**	*six*
d**ix**	*ten*

The Combinations *ied, ieds, ier, iers*

These are all pronounced like the English word *yay*. The vowel **i** produces a **yod** sound because it is followed by the vowel **e**. Review Lesson One.

$$[je]$$

EXAMPLES

(le) **pied**	*foot*
(les) **pieds**	*feet*
(le) pap**ier**	*paper*
(le) cah**ier**	*notebook*

But in h**ier** *(yesterday)* **i** is pronounced like *y* in the English word *yes* plus the sound of the English word *air*. Do not pronounce the **h**.

[je]

Examples

dern**ier**	*last* (m.s.)
prem**ier**	*first* (m.s.)
dern**iers**	*last* (m.pl.)
prem**iers**	*first* (m.pl.)
(les) cah**iers**	*notebooks*
(les) pap**iers**	*papers*

The Cluster *ième*

Pronounce this cluster like *y* in the English word *yes* plus the *e* as in the English word *egg* plus the **m** sound. This produces a sound like *yem*.

[jɛm]

Examples

deux**ième**	*second* (of more than two)
[The **x** in this word sounds like **z**.]	
douz**ième**	*twelfth*

The Clusters *ière, ières*

Pronounce these like *y* in the English word *yes* plus the sound of the English word *air*. These two clusters sound like the French word **hier** that you learned earlier.

[jɛːr]

Examples

prem**ière**	*first* (f.s.)
dern**ière**	*last* (f.s.)
(la) pr**ière**	*prayer*
(les) pr**ières**	*prayers*

The Combinations *il, ils*

In these two combinations, pronounce the vowel **i** plus the sound of **l**. Do not pronounce the **s**. They both sound something like the English word *eel*, except that the French consonant **l** is not pronounced exactly like the English *l*. See the consonant **l** in Lesson Seven.

[il]

EXAMPLES

il	*he, it*
(le) **cil**	*eyelash*
(le) **fil**	*thread*
ils	*they*
(les) **cils**	*eyelashes*
(les) **fils**	*threads*

In **le fils** *(son)* and **les fils** *(sons),* pronounce the **s** but do not pronounce the **l**. Both sound like *feess*.

[fis]

(le) **fils**	*son*
(les) **fils**	*sons*
Monsieur Albert a un **fils**.	*Mr. Albert has one son.* **(avoir)**
Madame Claire a deux **fils**.	*Mrs. Claire has two sons.* **(avoir)**

In the following two words, pronounce **s** like **z** plus the **i** sound. But do not pronounce the **l** or the final **s**. They both sound something like *few-zee*.

[fy′zi]

(le) fus**il**	*rifle*
(les) fus**ils**	*rifles*

Do the same for the following two words. They both sound something like *oo-tee*.

[u ´ti]

(l') out**il**	*tool*
(les) out**ils**	*tools*

In the following two words, do not pronounce **l** or **s.** The endings **til** and **tils** both sound like *tee.*

[ʒã´ti]

gent**il**	*nice, kind* (m.s.)
gent**ils**	*nice, kind* (m.pl.)

The Clusters *ille, illes*

In these two clusters, pronounce the vowel **i** as in the English word *see* plus the y sound (the **yod**) as in the English word *yes.*

[iːj]

EXAMPLES

(la) céd**ille**	*cedilla*
(la) f**ille**	*daughter*
(la) fam**ille**	*family*
gent**ille**	*nice, kind* (f.s.)
(les) céd**illes**	*cedillas*
(les) f**illes**	*daughters*
(les) fam**illes**	*families*
gent**illes**	*nice, kind* (f.pl.)

In the following two words, pronounce **i** plus single **l.** They both sound something like *veel.*

[vil]

(la) v**ille**	*city*
(les) v**illes**	*cities*

The Clusters *ique, iques*

These two clusters sound like *eek*.

$$[ik]$$

EXAMPLES

pacif**ique**	*pacific; peaceful, quiet*
(l') élast**ique**	*rubber band*
(la) bout**ique**	*small shop, boutique*
(les) élast**iques**	*rubber bands*
(les) bout**iques**	*small shops, boutiques*

Practice for Mastery

The speaker will now review all the combinations and clusters featuring the vowel **i.**

Note: These examples, which are not listed here, appeared earlier in this lesson. Just listen and repeat each word or group of words after the speaker.

Now go back to the beginning of the track and replay the review of 14 words or pairs of words numbered 1 to 14. This time, with a pencil, circle what you hear in each of the numbered pairs. This is a quiz on sound differentiation.

EXERCISE

1. **je dis**	**jeudi**		8. **le nid**	**le nez**
2. **deuxième**	**douzième**		9. **le fil**	**le fils**
3. **gentil**	**gentille**		10. **la fille**	**la ville**
4. **premier**	**première**		11. **joli**	**je lis**
5. **le prix**	**le riz**		12. **les îles**	**les cils**
6. **il lit**	**le lit**		13. **dernier**	**dernière**
7. **le cahier**	**hier**		14. **il dit**	**elle dit**

Play the track again and check your answers before looking at the answers in the box on page 56.

ANSWERS

1. je dis	**8.** le nid
2. douzième	**9.** le fils
3. gentil	**10.** la fille
4. première	**11.** je lis
5. le prix	**12.** les cils
6. le lit	**13.** dernier
7. hier	**14.** il dit

In the following words, if the last letter of the word is pronounced, circle YES. If it is not, circle NO.

EXERCISE

1. **le nid**	YES NO	5. **il**	YES NO
2. **le lis**	YES NO	6. **ils**	YES NO
3. **le lit**	YES NO	7. **le fil**	YES NO
4. **gris**	YES NO	8. **le fils**	YES NO

ANSWERS

1. NO	**3.** NO	**5.** YES	**7.** YES
2. YES	**4.** NO	**6.** NO	**8.** YES

Practice in Context

Now listen to a dialogue in which several combinations and clusters containing the vowel **i** are used. During the pauses, repeat each sentence or phrase after the speaker.

Mimi: Bonjour, Fifi!

Fifi: Bonjour, Mimi!

Mimi: Où vas-tu?

Fifi: Je vais en ville. J'ai des courses à faire dans les boutiques. Je vais à la boucherie et à la pâtisserie.

Mimi: Hello, Fifi!

Fifi: Hello, Mimi!

Mimi: Where are you going?

Fifi: I'm going downtown. I have some shopping to do in the little shops. I'm going to the butcher shop and to the pastry shop.

Mimi: Où est ton fils Philippe? Il est si gentil! Comment va-t-il?

Fifi: Il est à la maison. Il lit dans le lit.

Mimi: Et ta fille Monique? Elle est si gentille!

Fifi: Elle est allée acheter une paire de souliers gris. Et toi, Mimi, où vas-tu?

Mimi: Je vais acheter du riz. Le prix du riz ces jours-ci! Oh! C'est terrible!

Fifi: Oh, je sais! C'est la vie!

Mimi: Where is your son Philip? He is so nice! How is he?

Fifi: He's at home. He's reading in bed.

Mimi: And your daughter Monique? She is so nice!

Fifi: She went to buy a pair of gray shoes. And you, Mimi, where are you going?

Mimi: I'm going to buy some rice. The price of rice these days! Oh! It's terrible!

Fifi: Oh, I know! That's life!

Introducing the Sounds Featuring the Vowel *o* (A)

Listen carefully to all the examples, repeat the French words or phrases after the speaker, then listen for the confirmation.

The Cluster *oeil*

Pronounce this cluster like the *u* in the English word *curl* plus the *y* sound in the English word *yes*. When pronouncing it, thrust the lips a bit forward.

$$[œj]$$

EXAMPLES

(l') **oeil**	*eye*
(l') **oeil**lade	*glance; wink*
(l') **oeil**let	*carnation*

The Clusters *oeu, oeux, oeud, oeuds*

Pronounce these clusters like **eux** in **les cheveux,** which you learned earlier under the combination **eu.** Thrust the lips a bit forward.

$$[ø]$$

EXAMPLES

[vø]	(le) v**oeu**	*wish*
	(les) v**oeux**	*wishes*
	meilleurs v**oeux**	*best wishes*
[nø]	(le) n**oeud**	*knot*
	(les) n**oeuds**	*knots*

The Cluster *oeuf*

Pronounce this cluster like **euf** in **neuf** and **veuf,** which you learned earlier under the combination **eu.** Pronounce the **f.** Thrust the lips a bit forward while pronouncing it.

$$[œf]$$

EXAMPLES

(l') **oeuf**	*egg*
(le) b**oeuf**	*beef; ox*

In the plural form, **les oeufs** *(eggs)* and **les boeufs** *(pl. of beef; oxen)*, the **f** is not pronounced. Also note that the pronunciation of **oeu** changes to the sound of **eux** in **deux, feux, cheveux,** which you learned earlier under the combination **eu.** While pronouncing this sound, the lips are slightly forward but closer together than when you pronounce the singular **oeuf.**

$$[ø]$$

[lezø]	(les) **oeufs**	*eggs*
[lebø]	(les) b**oeufs**	*oxen;* pl. of *beef*

The Cluster *oeur*

Pronounce this cluster like *ur* in the English word *curl*. In fact, it sounds very much like *curl* without the *l* sound. When pronouncing it, thrust your lips forward a little.

$$[œːr]$$

EXAMPLES

[kœːr]

(le) c**oeur**	*heart*	
(le) Sacré-C**oeur**	*Sacred Heart* (name	
	of church in Paris)	

[sœːr]

(la) s**oeur**	*sister*
(la) belle-s**oeur**	*sister-in-law*

The Cluster *oeuvre*

This cluster is pronounced like **oeu** in **oeuf** (which you learned earlier). Pronounce the **v** and the **r** sounds but not the **e**.

$$[œːvr]$$

EXAMPLES

(l') **oeuvre**	*work*
(l') **oeuvre** d'art	*work of art*
(les) hors-d'**oeuvre**	*appetizers*
(le) chef-d'**oeuvre**	*masterpiece*

Do not pronounce the **f** in **chef-d'oeuvre**. The proper pronunciation in IPA symbols is written like this: **[lə ʃɛ ˈdœːvr]**. The plural of this word is written as **les chefs-d'oeuvre,** but the pronunciation remains the same as in the singular except that the definite article **le** must change to **les.** Remember that the mark ´ indicates that the stress (raise your voice a bit) falls on the syllable *after* it. And you must remember by now that the mark ː indicates that the vowel sound *in front of it* is long (stretched out a bit). Try pronouncing the

singular and plural of this word at least three times at the same time as you write the words. The **f** in **chef** is pronounced when the word means *boss* or *chief,* as in **chef de cuisine,** *head cook in a kitchen.*

The Combinations *oi, oid, oids, oie, oigt, ois, oit, oix, oua*

These are all pronounced *wa* like in the English word *watt.*

[wa]

EXAMPLES

m**oi**	*me*
t**oi**	*you*
s**oi**	*oneself*
(le) s**oir**	*evening*
	[Pronounce the **r** in **soir.**]
(la) s**oirée**	*evening; evening party*
(la) l**oi**	*law*
(la) f**oi**	*faith*
(le) r**oi**	*king*
(la) s**oif**	*thirst*
	[Pronounce the **f** in **soif.**]
n**oir**	*black*
	[Pronounce the **r** in **noir.** It rhymes with **soir.**]
(la) p**oire**	*pear*
(le) p**oireau**	*leek*
(les) p**oireaux**	*leeks*
	[Note that **poireau** and **poireaux** both sound exactly like the name **Poirot,** the criminologist extraordinaire in Agatha Christie's mystery novels. See the combination **ot** farther on.]
(le) fr**oid**	*cold*

(le) p**oids**	*weight*
(l') **oie**	*goose*
(le) f**oie**	*liver*
(la) s**oie**	*silk*
(le) d**oigt**	*finger*
(la) f**ois**	*time*
(la) première f**ois**	*first time*
(la) dernière f**ois**	*last time*
(le) m**ois**	*month*
(le) p**ois**	*pea*
je d**ois**	*I must* (**devoir**)
je cr**ois**	*I believe* (**croire**)
je b**ois**	*I drink, I am drinking* (**boire**)
je v**ois**	*I see, I am seeing* (**voir**)
(le) t**oit**	*roof*
il d**oit**	*he must* (**devoir**)
elle cr**oit**	*she believes* (**croire**)
(la) cr**oix**	*cross*
(la) n**oix**	*walnut*
	[Do not pronounce **oi** as *wa* in **l'oignon** (onion). It is pronounced as *u* in the English word *up*.]
(la) **ouat**e	*padding; cotton wool*
	[This sounds very much like the English word *watt*.]
ouaté	*padded; quilted*
ouater	*to pad; to quilt*

Note: In the present subjunctive verb form **soit** (**être**), meaning *be*, the letter **t** is not pronounced. But the **t** is pronounced emphatically in **soit!** and it means *so be it!*

The Clusters *omme, ommes*

These are both pronounced *um* as in the English word *plum*.

[ɔm]

EXAMPLES

c**omme**	*as, like*
(la) s**omme**	*sum, amount*
(le) s**omme**	*nap, snooze*
(l') h**omme**	*man*
(les) h**ommes**	*men*
(la) p**omme**	*apple*
(les) p**ommes**	*apples*
nous s**ommes**	*we are*

The Cluster *omne*

This is pronounced *un* as in the English word *ton*. The **m** is not pronounced, but the **n** is pronounced.

$$[ɔn]$$

EXAMPLE

(l') aut**omne**	*autumn, fall*

The Combination *one*

This is pronounced *un* as in the English word *fun*.

$$[ɔn]$$

EXAMPLES

(le) téléph**one**	*telephone*
je téléph**one**	*I telephone, I am telephoning* **(téléphoner)**
angloph**one**	*English-speaking*
francoph**one**	*French-speaking*
monot**one**	*monotonous*

The Cluster *onne*

This spelling is also pronounced *un* as in the English word *bun*.

$$[\text{ɔn}]$$

EXAMPLES

b**onne**	*good* (f.s.)
(la) b**onne**	*maid*
je d**onne**	*I give, I am giving* **(donner)**
(la) t**onne**	*ton*
(la) pers**onne**	*person*
(la) cour**onne**	*crown*
le téléphone s**onne**	*the telephone is ringing* **(sonner)**

The Combination *op*

When this combination is the ending of a word, it is normally pronounced *o* as in the English word *over*. But be careful! Do not bring the lips together in order to avoid pronouncing that slight *w* sound.

$$[\text{o}]$$

EXAMPLES

(le) gal**op**	*gallop*
(le) sir**op**	*syrup*
tr**op**	*too, too much, too many*

Note that the **p** is pronounced in the expression **allez, hop!** Do not pronounce the **h**.

It can mean *come on! upsadaisy! hop to it! let's get on with it!*

$$[\text{ale ´ɔp}]$$

The Combination os

When this combination is the ending of a word, it is normally pronounced as a closed *o*. Do not pronounce the *s*.

[o]

EXAMPLES

à prop**os**	*by the way*
(le) d**os**	*back* (of a person)
(le) cha**os**	*chaos*
	[Pronounce **ch** like *k* in the English word *chaos*.]
(le) hér**os**	*hero*
	[Do not pronounce the **h** in **héros**.]
(le) rep**os**	*rest, repose*
gr**os**	*big, bulky, stout* (m.s.)
n**os**	*our* (pl. of **notre**)
v**os**	*your* (pl. of **votre**)

In the word **l'os** *(bone)* in the singular, pronounce **os** as the English word *us*. However, in the plural, **les os** *(bones)*, **os** is pronounced like *o* in the English word *over* without that slight *w* sound. In the plural, **les os** sounds exactly like **les eaux** *(waters)*, which you learned earlier under the **eau, eaux** combinations. Pronounce the **s** in **les** as *z* so it sounds like *lay-zo*.

[lɔs]
[le ´zo]

(l') **os**	*bone*
(les) **os**	*bones*

In the following word, pronounce **os** like the English word *us*.

[ɔs]

(l') albatr**os**	[alba´trɔ:s]	*albatross*

The Cluster osse

When this cluster is at the ending of a word, it is normally pronounced like the English word *us*.

[ɔs]

EXAMPLES

(l') Éc**osse**	*Scotland*
(la) b**osse**	*hump*
(le) g**osse**	*kid, youngster* (m.s.)
(la) g**osse**	*kid, youngster* (f.s.)

The word **gosse** sounds like the English name *Gus*. But **osse** in the following word is pronounced *os* as in the English word *host*.

[gros]

gr**osse**	*big, bulky* (f.s.; the m.s. is **gros** listed earlier under **os**.)

The Combination ot

When this combination is at the ending of a word, it is normally pronounced *o* as in the English word *over*. When pronouncing *o*, make sure you don't tack on that *w* sound.

[o]

EXAMPLES

(l') abric**ot**	*apricot*
(le) can**ot**	*open boat*
(le) tric**ot**	*knitted sweater*
(le) p**ot**	*pot; potty*
(le) m**ot**	*word*
Alfred Cort**ot**	(French pianist)

Exception: In the following word, **t** is pronounced and **o** sounds like *u* in the English word *but*.

| (la) d**ot** | [la dɔt] | *dowry* |

The Combination ôt

This combination sounds exactly like closed *o* in *over*.

[o]

t**ôt**	*early*
aussit**ôt**	*at once, immediately*
bient**ôt**	*soon*
à bient**ôt**	*see you soon*
plut**ôt**	*rather*

The Cluster otte

This cluster is pronounced like *ut* in the English word *but*.

[ɔt]

EXAMPLES

(la) b**otte**	*boot; bunch*
(la) b**otte** de fleurs	*bunch of flowers*
(la) car**otte**	*carrot*
(la) jupe-cul**otte**	*culotte skirt*
(la) fl**otte**	*fleet*

Practice for Mastery

The speaker will now review all the combinations and clusters featuring the vowel **o**.

Note: These examples, which are not listed here, appeared earlier in this lesson. Just listen and repeat each word or group of words after the speaker.

Now go back to the beginning of the track and replay the review of 20 words or groups of words numbered 1 to 20. This time, with a pencil, circle what you hear in each of the numbered pairs. This is a quiz on sound differentiation.

EXERCISE

1. **oeil**	**aile**	11. **froid**	**frais**
2. **nez**	**noeud**	12. **homme**	**aime**
3. **les boeufs**	**le boeuf**	13. **sonné**	**sonne**
4. **coeur**	**car**	14. **dos**	**des**
5. **veau**	**voeu**	15. **gros**	**grosse**
6. **l'oeuf**	**les oeufs**	16. **canot**	**canoë**
7. **sur**	**soeur**	17. **sot**	**sotte**
8. **oeuvre**	**ouvre**	18. **flotte**	**flot**
9. **moi**	**mes**	19. **trop**	**très**
10. **peur**	**poire**	20. **l'oeil**	**les yeux**

Play the track again and check your answers before looking at the answers in the box.

ANSWERS

1. oeil	8. oeuvre	15. grosse
2. noeud	9. moi	16. canot
3. le boeuf	10. poire	17. sotte
4. coeur	11. froid	18. flotte
5. voeu	12. homme	19. trop
6. l'oeuf	13. sonne	20. l'oeil
7. soeur	14. dos	

In the following words, if the last consonant of the word is pronounced, circle YES. If it is not, circle NO.

EXERCISE

1. **boeuf**	YES NO		5. **froid**	YES NO
2. **coeur**	YES NO		6. **soeur**	YES NO
3. **oeufs**	YES NO		7. **flot**	YES NO
4. **voeux**	YES NO		8. **sommes**	YES NO

ANSWERS

1. YES	**3.** NO	**5.** NO	**7.** NO
2. YES	**4.** NO	**6.** YES	**8.** NO

Practice in Context

Now listen to a monologue in which several combinations and clusters containing the vowel **o** are used. During the pauses, repeat each sentence or phrase after the speaker.

Je suis dans un bistrot appelé *Au chef d'oeuvre.*

I am in a small café called At the Masterpiece.

J'ai soif.

I'm thirsty.

Je bois un café noir.

I'm drinking black coffee.

Il est trop sucré.

It is too sweet.

L'homme derrière le comptoir est gros.

The man behind the counter is big.

Il a les bras gros et les mains grosses.

He has big arms and big hands.

Je lui demande un oeuf dur, du poivre et du sel.

I ask him for a hard-boiled egg, some pepper and some salt.

Il me regarde d'un oeil froid et il demande à sa femme s'il y a des oeufs durs.

He looks at me with a cold eye and he asks his wife if there are any hard-boiled eggs.

Elle répond qu'il n'y en a plus en ajustant une petite couronne de petits oeillets sur la tête.

She answers that there aren't any more while adjusting a little crown of small carnations on her head.

Elle est bizarre.

She is strange.

Je bois mon café noir, je mets trois euros sur le comptoir, et je pars.

I drink my black coffee, I place three euros on the counter, and I leave.

Introducing the Sounds Featuring the Vowel o (B)

Listen carefully to all the examples, repeat the French words or phrases after the speaker, then listen for the confirmation.

The Combinations ou, où

These two combinations are pronounced *oo* as in the English word *soon*. The **accent grave** on **ù** in **où** is written to distinguish its meaning from the word **ou**. That is the only word in the French language that contains this accent mark on the vowel **u**.

[u]

EXAMPLES

ou	*or*
où	*where*
(le) gen**ou**	*knee*
(le) c**ou**	*neck*
f**ou**	*crazy*
(le) ch**ou**	*cabbage*
(le) ch**ou**-fleur	*cauliflower*
(le) c**ou**de	*elbow*
t**ou**cher	*to touch*
p**ou**sser	*to push*
t**ou**sser	*to cough*
(le) ya**ou**rt	*yogurt*

The Combinations oue, ouls, oup, ous, out, oût, oux

These spellings are also pronounced *oo* as in the English word *soon*.

[u]

EXAMPLES

(la) b**oue**	*mud*
(la) j**oue**	*cheek*
je j**oue**	*I play* **(jouer)**
(le) p**ouls**	*pulse*
(le) l**oup**	*wolf*

(le) c**oup**	*hit, blow*
(le) c**oup** d'état	*overthrow of the government*
(le) c**oup** de pied	*kick*
beauc**oup**	*much, many*
s**ous**	*under*
dess**ous**	*underneath*
t**ous**	*all* (m.pl.)

[When the word **tous** is an adjective, do not pronounce the **s**, as in **tous les livres** *all the books*. But when **tous** is a pronoun, pronounce the **s**, as in **ils sont tous ici** *they are all here*.]

f**ous**	*crazy* (m.pl.)
v**ous**	*you*
n**ous**	*we; us*
t**out**	*all* (m.s.)
t**out** à coup	*suddenly*
t**out** d'un coup	*all of a sudden*
deb**out**	*standing*
part**out**	*everywhere*
surt**out**	*above all, especially*
(le) c**oût**	*cost*
(le) g**oût**	*taste*
(le) dég**oût**	*disgust*
(le) rag**oût**	*stew*
a**oût**	*August*
	[It is also correct to pronounce the **t** in **août**.]

[lə u]

(la) t**oux**	*cough*
(le) h**oux**	*holly*
(les) p**oux**	*lice*
(l') ép**oux**	*husband; spouse*

[Note that **les poux** and **l'époux** are both pronounced the same. Of course, when they are used, you can tell the difference in meaning from the context.]

d**oux**	*soft; sweet* (m.s.)
jal**oux**	*jealous* (m.s.)
(les) gen**oux**	*knees*

The Clusters *ouille, ouilles*

These clusters are both pronounced *oo* plus the *y* sound as in the English word *yes*, which is expressed in the phonetic symbol [j].

$$[u:j]$$

EXAMPLES

(la) n**ouille**	noodle
(la) gren**ouille**	frog
(la) citr**ouille**	pumpkin
(les) n**ouilles**	noodles
(les) gren**ouilles**	frogs
(les) citr**ouilles**	pumpkins

The Combinations *our, ourd, ours, ourds*

These are all pronounced *oor* as in the English word *poor*. Do not pronounce the final **s**.

$$[u:r]$$

EXAMPLES

[lə tu:r]

	p**our**	for
(le)	f**our**	oven
(l')	am**our**	love
(le)	j**our**	day
(la)	t**our**	tower
(le)	t**our**	turn
	l**ourd**	heavy (m.s.)
	l**ourds**	heavy (m.pl.)
(les)	f**ours**	ovens
(les)	am**ours**	loves
(les)	j**ours**	days

In the following three words, pronounce the **s.**

[lurs]	(l') **ours**	bear
[le´zurs]	(les) **ours**	bears
[lə nu´nurs]	(le) **nounours**	teddy bear

Practice for Mastery

The speaker will now continue to review additional combinations and clusters featuring the vowel **o.** This is the conclusion of that section.

Note: These examples, not listed here, appeared earlier in this lesson. Just listen and repeat each word or group of words after the speaker.

Now, go back to the beginning of the track and replay the review of ten words numbered 1 to 10. This time, with a pencil, circle what you hear in each of the numbered pairs. This is a quiz on sound differentiation.

EXERCISE

1. **cou**	coude	6. **lourds**	lourde
2. **jour**	jure	7. **pouls**	pu
3. **sous**	su	8. **bu**	boue
4. **tu**	tout	9. **tout à coup**	tout d'un coup
5. **pour**	pur	10. **joue**	jouer

Play the track again and check your answers before looking at the answers in the box.

ANSWERS

1. cou	**5.** pour	**9.** tout à coup
2. jour	**6.** lourds	**10.** joue
3. sous	**7.** pouls	
4. tout	**8.** boue	

In the following words, if the last consonant of the word is pronounced, circle YES. If it is not, circle NO.

EXERCISE

1. **sous**	YES NO	5. **amour**	YES NO
2. **yaourt**	YES NO	6. **pouls**	YES NO
3. **four**	YES NO	7. **époux**	YES NO
4. **vous**	YES NO	8. **ours**	YES NO

ANSWERS

1. NO	**3.** YES	**5.** YES	**7.** NO
2. NO	**4.** NO	**6.** NO	**8.** YES

Practice in Context

Now listen to a dialogue in which several combinations and clusters containing the vowel **o** are used. During the pauses, repeat each sentence or phrase after the speaker.

Le serveur: Bonsoir. Qu'est-ce que vous désirez commander?

Waiter: Good evening. What do you wish to order?

Madame: Pour moi, j'aimerais le ragoût. Et toi, mon amour?

Madam: For me, I'd like the stew. And you, my love?

Monsieur: J'aimerais aussi le ragoût. Et un plat de nouilles au beurre. Y a-t-il du chou-fleur?

Sir: I'd like the stew also. And a plate of buttered noodles. Is there any cauliflower?

Le serveur: Mais oui, monsieur.

Waiter: Of course, sir.

Monsieur: Bon, alors, apportez-moi un plat de chou-fleur au gratin.

Sir: Good, then, bring me a plate of cauliflower cooked with grated cheese.

Le serveur: C'est tout, monsieur?

Waiter: Is that all, sir?

Monsieur: Non. J'adore le yaourt. Y en a-t-il?

Sir: No. I love yogurt. Is there any?

Le serveur: Mais oui, monsieur. Nous avons du yaourt.

Monsieur: Bon, alors, du yaourt aussi. Et comme dessert, un plat de petits-fours. Et puis, apportez-moi . . .

Madame: Je crois que cela suffit, mon amour. Si tu manges trop, tu deviendras gros comme un ours!

Waiter: Of course, sir. We have yogurt.

Sir: Good, then, some yogurt too. And for dessert, a plate of little glazed cakes. And then, bring me . . .

Madam: I believe that is sufficient, my love. If you eat too much, you'll become fat as a bear!

Introducing the Sounds Featuring the Vowel *u*

Listen carefully to all the examples, repeat the French words or phrases after the speaker, then listen for the confirmation.

The Clusters *ueil, ueils, ueille, ueilles*

These four clusters all sound the same. Pronounce **ue** the same as **eu** in the French word **heure** that you learned earlier under the combination **eu.** It sounds something like the *u* in the English word *curl.* Then add the slight *y* sound in the word *yes.*

As a matter of fact, these four clusters sound the same as **euil, euils, euille, euilles** that you learned previously, but note that **eu** is reversed to **ue.** The two vowels are reversed because of the consonant **c,** which is pronounced like **k** before the vowel **u.** Review the clusters **euil, euils, euille, euilles** in the section under the combination **eu.** You will see that the consonant **c** does not precede them. But in these four clusters, the consonant **c** causes **eu** to change to **ue.**

$$[\text{œ :j}]$$

EXAMPLES

(l') acc**ueil**	*reception, welcome*
(les) acc**ueils**	*receptions, welcomes*
acc**ueil**lir un ami	*to welcome a friend*

Tu acc**ueilles** tes amis?	*Do you welcome your friends?*
Je c**ueille** des roses.	*I'm gathering roses.*
c**ueill**ir	*to gather, to pick*
(le) c**ueill**eur de fleurs	*flower picker, gatherer (m.s.)*
(la) c**ueill**euse de fruits	*fruit picker, gatherer (f.s.)*
(le) rec**ueil**	*anthology, collection*
(les) rec**ueils**	*anthologies, collections*

Practice for Mastery

The speaker will now review the combinations and clusters featuring the vowel **u**.

Note: These examples, not listed here, appeared earlier in this lesson. Just listen and repeat each word or group of words after the speaker.

Now go back to the beginning of the track and replay the review of six words or groups of words numbered 1 to 6. This time, with a pencil, circle what you hear in each of the numbered pairs. This is a quiz on sound differentiation.

EXERCISE

1. **accueil**	**recueil**
2. **cueilleur**	**cueilleuse**
3. **cueille**	**accueils**
4. **cueillir**	**cueilles**
5. **je cueille**	**j'accueille**
6. **tu accueilles**	**tu accueilles?**

Play the track again and check your answers before looking at the answers in the box.

ANSWERS

1. accueil	**3.** cueille	**5.** j'accueille
2. cueilleuse	**4.** cueillir	**6.** tu accueilles?

Practice in Context

Now listen to a monologue in which several combinations and clusters containing the vowel **u** are used. During the pauses, repeat each sentence or phrase after the speaker.

Avez-vous jamais été accueilli aimablement? C'est bon. Avez-vous jamais été accueilli froidement? Ce n'est pas bon! Chaque fois que je vais chez mes amis, ils m'accueillent chaleureusement. Ils me font toujours bon accueil . . . Je vois que vous cueillez des roses. Avez-vous cueilli toutes les roses qui sont dans ce vase? Cueillez, cueillez les roses de la vie!

Have you ever been welcomed kindly? It's good. Have you ever been welcomed coldly? It's not good! Each time I go to my friends' homes, they welcome me warmly. They always give me a good welcome . . . I see you're gathering some roses. Did you pick all the roses that are in this vase? Gather, gather the roses of life!

Introducing the Sounds Featuring the Semivowel *y*

Listen carefully to all the examples, repeat the French words or phrases after the speaker, then listen for the confirmation. Review Lesson One.

The Combinations *aye, ayes*

Pronounce both like *e* in the English word *bell* plus a slight *y* sound as in the English word *yes*.

$$[\varepsilon j]$$

EXAMPLES

je p**aye**	*I pay, I am paying*
tu p**ayes**	*you pay, you are paying* (**payer**)

Note that verbs ending in **ayer** may change the **y** to **i** before mute (silent) **e** or may keep the **y,** as in the two verb forms of the verb **payer** *(to pay).* When **y** changes to **i,** the **yod** sound disappears and **aie** or **aies** are both pronounced like *e* in the English word *bell.*

$$[\varepsilon]$$

| je p**aie** | *I pay, I am paying* |
| tu p**aies** | *you pay, you are paying* **(payer)** |

The Combination *ayer*

Pronounce **ay** like *e* in the English word *bell* plus a slight **yod** sound plus *a* as in the English word *ate.* Here the vowel **e** is not a mute (silent) **e** because it goes with **er.**

$$[\varepsilon \ ´je]$$

EXAMPLES

p**ayer**	*to pay*
bal**ayer**	*to sweep*
bég**ayer**	*to stammer, to stutter*
ess**ayer**	*to try*

The Combination *ayez*

Pronounce **ayez** like **ayer** earlier.

$$[\varepsilon \ ´je]$$

EXAMPLES

vous p**ayez**	*you pay, you are paying*
vous bal**ayez**	*you sweep, you are sweeping*
vous bég**ayez**	*you stutter, you are stuttering*
vous ess**ayez**	*you try, you are trying*
que vous **ayez**	*that you may have* **(avoir)**

The Combination *ays*

Pronounce **ay** like *ay* in the English word *pay* plus the sound *ee* as in the English word *see*. Do not pronounce the **s**. The French word **pays** sounds very much like the English word *payee*.

[ei]

EXAMPLES

(le) **pay**s	country
(le) **pay**sage	countryside

The Combination *ey*

Pronounce **ey** like *e* in the English word *egg*.

[ɛ]

EXAMPLES

[ʒɔˈkɛ]
[diskʒɔˈkɛ]
[vɔˈlɛ]

(le) jock**ey**	*jockey*
(le) disc-jock**ey**	*disk jockey*
(le) voll**ey**	*volley*

The Combination *oyer*

Pronounce **oy** like *wa* in the English word *watt* plus a slight **yod** sound plus the *a* sound in *ate*.

[wa ´je]

EXAMPLES

empl**oyer**	*to employ, to use*
env**oyer**	*to send*
nett**oyer**	*to clean*
n**oyer**	*to drown*
tut**oyer**	*(to use the familiar **tu** verb form)*

vouv**oyer**	(to use the polite or plural **vous** verb form)
(le) f**oyer**	hearth; foyer
(le) l**oyer**	rent

The Combination *oyez*

Pronounce **oyez** like **oyer** earlier.

$$[wa´je]$$

EXAMPLES

vous empl**oyez**	you employ, you use
vous env**oyez**	you send, you are sending
vous nett**oyez**	you clean, you are cleaning

The Combination *uyer*

Pronounce **uy** like the English *you eat* without the *t* sound plus a slight **yod** sound plus the usual *ay* sound.

$$[ɥi´je]$$

EXAMPLES

| ess**uyer** | to wipe |
| enn**uyer** | to annoy, to bore, to bother |

The Combination *ya*

Pronounce **ya** a little like *ya* in the English word *yahoo!*

$$[ja]$$

EXAMPLES

| Ma**ya** | Maya |
| (le) **ya**ourt | yogurt |

The Cluster *yeux*

The **y** in this cluster is pronounced like the *y* in the English word *yes* plus the sound of *u* in the English word *pudding*, as in **eux** in the French word **deux,** which you learned earlier under the combination **eu.**

[jø]

EXAMPLES

(les) **yeux**	*eyes*
jo**yeux**	*joyful, joyous, merry*
Jo**yeux** Noël	*Merry Christmas*

The Combination *yod*

Pronounce **y** like the *y* in *yes* plus the sound of *u* in *up* plus the **d** sound. As you learned in this lesson and in previous ones, **le yod** is the French word for the semivowel sound of *y* in *yes*.

[jɔd]

The Combination *you*

Pronounce **you** like the English word *you*. Do not bring the lips together after the *oo* sound because that would produce a slight *w* sound.

[ju]

EXAMPLES

(la) **You**goslavie	*Yugoslavia*
(le) **voyou**	*street kid*
youpi!	*oh, boy!* (an exclamation that expresses joy)

Practice for Mastery

The speaker will now review all the combinations and clusters featuring the vowel **y**.

Note: These examples, not listed here, appeared earlier in this lesson. Just listen and repeat each word or group of words after the speaker.

Now go back to the beginning of the track and replay the review of six words or groups of words numbered 1 to 6. This time, with a pencil, circle what you hear in each of the numbered pairs. This is a quiz on sound differentiation.

EXERCISE

1. je paye	je paie	4. youyou	yo-yo
2. pays	payez	5. joyeux	joyeuse
3. essayer	essuyer	6. voyage	voyagé

Play the track again and check your answers before looking at the answers in the box.

ANSWERS

1. je paye	**3.** essayer	**5.** joyeux
2. pays	**4.** youyou	**6.** voyagé

Practice in Context

Now listen to a dialogue in which several combinations and clusters containing the semivowel **y** are used. During the pauses, repeat each sentence or phrase after the speaker.

Madame: Maya! Maya! Que faites-vous? Et à genoux!

Madam: Maya! Maya! What are you doing? And on your knees!

Maya: Ne voyez-vous pas, Madame Yvette? Je commence à nettoyer le foyer.

Maya: Don't you see, Madame Yvette? I'm beginning to clean the foyer.

Madame: Pourquoi nettoyez-vous le foyer maintenant? Je vous ai demandé d'aller chez le boulanger pour lui payer ce que je dois.

Maya: J'ai laissé tomber le pot de yaourt! Il est partout!

Madame: Essuyez la table aussi. Après le nettoyage, allez chercher les billets à l'agence de voyages pour mon voyage en Yougoslavie. Et essayez de ne pas prendre trop de temps.

Maya: Oui, madame. Tout de suite. J'irai à bicyclette.

Madame: Quelle bonne!

Madam: Why are you cleaning the foyer now? I asked you to go to the baker to pay him what I owe.

Maya: I dropped the container of yogurt! It's everywhere!

Madam: Wipe the table too. After cleaning up, go get the tickets at the travel agency for my trip to Yugoslavia. And try not to take too much time.

Maya: Yes, madam. Right away. I'll go on my bicycle.

Madam: What a maid!

LESSON FOUR
THE THREE SEMIVOWELS

Introducing the Sounds

Listen carefully to all the examples, repeat the French words or phrases after the speaker, then listen for the confirmation.

There are three semivowel sounds in French:

1. the **yod** sound that you learned in previous sections in a variety of spellings.

[j]

EXAMPLES

[lə l j ø]

[v ɛːj]

[la f iːj]

(le) **lieu**	*place*
(le) p**ied**	*foot*
(l') **oeil**	*eye*
(la) v**eille**	*eve*
(la) v**eille** de Noël	*Christmas Eve*
v**ieille**	*old* (f.s.)
(la) f**ille**	*daughter*
(la) jeune f**ille**	*girl*
(les) **yeux**	*eyes*
(la) ma**yo**nnaise	*mayonnaise*

2. **u** + **i** produces a sound similar to the sound of *you eat* (the *t* is not pronounced). But be careful! Do not round your lips when you say *you* because you will produce a *w* sound.

[ɥi]

EXAMPLES

[lч i l]

[ʒə sчi]

[də´pчi]

[чit]

	(l') huile	*oil*
	lui	*him, to him, to her*
	je suis	*I am* (**être**)
	(la) cuisine	*kitchen*
	faire la cuisine	*to cook* (**faire**)
	depuis	*since*
	juillet	*July*
	(la) nuit	*night*
	huit	*eight*

Pronounce the **t** in **huit.** But do not pronounce the **t** if the word that follows begins with a consonant.

[чi mwa]

huit mois	*eight months*

Note that **u + y** produces the same sound.

[чi]

[ãnчi´je]

appuyer	*to lean, to press*
ennuyer	*to bore, to bother*
essuyer	*to wipe*

3. There are times when **ou** produces a *w* sound.

[w]

EXAMPLES

[wi]

[ʒwɛ]

	oui	*yes*
	ouest	*west*
	louer	*to praise; to rent*
	Louis	*Louis*
	Louise	*Louise*
	jouer	*to play*
	(le) jouet	*toy*

Practice for Mastery

The speaker will now review all the examples featuring the semivowel sounds.

Note: These examples, not listed here, appeared earlier in this lesson. Just listen and repeat each word or group of words after the speaker.

Now listen to the track again and replay the review of eight words numbered 1 to 8. This time, with a pencil, circle what you hear in each of the numbered pairs. This is a quiz on sound differentiation.

EXERCISE

1. **veille**	vieille	5. **nuit**	huit
2. **lui**	Louis	6. **louer**	luire
3. **suis**	suisse	7. **les jeux**	les yeux
4. **oeil**	huile	8. **appuyer**	appeler

Play the track again and check your answers before looking at the answers in the box.

ANSWERS

1. vieille	3. suis	5. nuit	7. les yeux
2. lui	4. huile	6. louer	8. appuyer

Practice in Context

Now listen to a monologue in which several words are used containing semivowel sounds. During the pauses, repeat each sentence or phrase after the speaker.

Je suis Louise Luisant.

I am Louise Luisant.

J'habite une vieille maison depuis dix-huit ans avec mon mari Louis.

I've been living in an old house for eighteen years with my husband Louis.

J'ai les yeux gris; il a les yeux bleus.

I have gray eyes; his eyes are blue.

Nous avons, tous les deux, les cheveux gris.

We both have gray hair.

J'aime faire la cuisine avec de l'huile d'olive.

I like to cook with olive oil.

Après le dîner, nous aimons jouer aux cartes.

After dinner, we like to play cards.

De temps en temps, notre petite-fille Louise nous rend visite et nous adorons la voir jouer avec ses jouets.

From time to time, our grand-daughter Louise visits us and we love to see her play with her toys.

Quand je lui demande si elle aime ses jouets, elle répond, "Oui, oui."

When I ask her if she likes her toys, she answers, "Yes, yes."

Introducing the Sounds

Listen carefully to all the examples, repeat the French words or phrases after the speaker, then listen for the confirmation.

There are four nasal vowel sounds in French. At one time, there were more than four, but through the centuries some of them have disappeared from use. One of the four (**un** or **um**) is rarely used in the city of Paris and its environs or in the western part of France. It has been replaced by one of the remaining three. In other regions of France, however, it is still in use.

Ordinarily, an oral vowel is nasalized when it is followed by **m** or **n** *in the same syllable.* An oral vowel is pronounced only through the mouth, which you learned in preceding lessons. A nasal vowel, however, is pronounced through the nose *and* through the mouth *at the same time* by pushing the breath up the nose and out of the mouth. To form a nasal vowel, you must first position your lips for its equivalent oral vowel, then nasalize it. The position must be precise to obtain the correct sound.

In the examples that follow, the oral vowels and nasal vowels are in **bold type.** The oral vowels do not contain **m** or **n** after them but the nasal vowels do. First, position the lips for the oral vowel sound given in each example, then nasalize it.

Oral Vowel Sound [œ]

EXAMPLE

[la flœːr]

| (la) fl**eur** | *flower* |

First Nasal Vowel Sound [œ̃]

EXAMPLES

un	*a, an, one (m.s.)*
(le) **lun**di	*Monday*
(le) par**fum**	*perfume*

The nasal vowel sound in the spellings **un** and **um** is the one rarely used in Paris or in the western region of France. In those areas, it is now pronounced like the nasal vowel sound in the spellings **in** or **im.** See the word **vin** under the **Third Nasal Vowel Sound** on page 90.

Review the sound of the oral vowel **eu** in **leur, fleur, bonheur, peur** under the combination **eu** in Lesson Three. You must position the lips properly to pronounce the oral vowel **eu** in those words, somewhat like the *u* when you pronounce the English word *curl.* The lips are parted and thrust slightly forward. Then nasalize the **eu** sound. It will produce the nasal vowel sound of **un** or **um.** (See Figure 10.)

[œ̃]

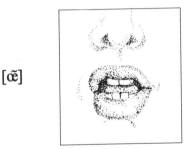

Figure 10.
The Nasal Vowel Sound of **un, um.**

Oral Vowel Sound [o]

EXAMPLE

b**eau**	*beautiful (m.s.)*

Second Nasal Vowel Sound [õ]

EXAMPLES

	b**on**	*good*
(les)	b**on**b**ons**	*candies; goodies*
	m**on**	*my*
	n**on**	*no*
(le)	n**om**	*name*
(la)	b**om**be	*bomb*

Review the oral sound of the combination **eau,** which sounds like *o* in the English word *over*. Other examples are **bateau** and **chapeau.** They are listed under the combinations **eau** and **eaux** in Lesson Three. You must position the lips properly to pronounce the sound of the oral vowel **o** in those words. Review the vowel **o** in Lesson One. With the lips in that position, nasalize the **o.** It will produce the nasal vowel sound of **on** or **om.** For practice, first pronounce **beau,** then pronounce **bon.** (See Figure 11.)

[õ]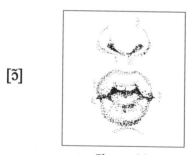

Figure 11.
The Nasal Vowel Sound of **on, om.**

Some words contain the vowel **o** plus double **m** but are *not* nasalized because the words are of one syllable and they end in a mute (silent) **e** or silent **s:** for example, **pomme** *(apple)*, **pommes** *(apples)*. The pronunciation of **omme** and **ommes** sounds like *um* in the English word *umbrella*. Those two French words, and others, are in Lesson Three under **omme** and **ommes.** Go back and listen to them again.

Some words contain the vowel **o** plus double **n** but are *not* nasalized either because the words are of one syllable and end in a mute (silent) **e**: for example, b**onne**, d**onne**, t**onne**. The sound of **onne** in those three words is like the sound of *un* in the English words *bun, done, ton*. Those three French words, and others, are in Lesson Three under **onne**. Go back and listen to them again. For practice, first pronounce **bon,** then **bonne; don,** then **donne; ton,** then **tonne.**

The combination **on** is nasalized, as in **bon** and **mon,** but when the vowel **e** is after it, that final **e** denasalizes **on,** as in **monotone** *(monotonous)*.

Let's divide the word **monotone** into syllables so you can understand why **mon** and **ton** are not nasalized in this word: **mo-no-tone.** As you can see, we cannot say a vowel is always nasal when followed by **m** or **n.** It depends on how the syllables are divided and whether **m** or **n** goes with the vowel in front of it or after it. The final **e** in **monotone** denasalizes **ton.** Review the French words under the combination **one** in Lesson Three where **monotone** and other French words are listed.

Oral Vowel Sound [ɛ]

EXAMPLES

je v**ais**	*I'm going* **(aller)**
je f**ais**	*I'm doing* **(faire)**
m**ais**	*but*
je s**ais**	*I know* **(savoir)**

Third Nasal Vowel Sound [ɛ̃]

EXAMPLES

(le) v**in**	*wine*
(la) f**in**	*end*
(la) f**aim**	*hunger*

(la) m**ain**	*hand*
rom**ain**	*Roman*
s**aint**	*saint*
s**im**ple	*simple*
(le) s**ein**	*breast*

This is the nasal sound that has absorbed the nasal vowel sound of the spellings **un** and **um** in Paris and its environs and in the western part of France, mentioned previously.

This nasal vowel contains a variety of spellings, as you can see in the list of examples. To produce the nasal vowel sound of **in, aim, ain, im, ein,** you must first pronounce the oral vowel combination **ais** properly that you learned in Lesson Three.

You must position your lips properly to pronounce the oral vowel combination **ais,** like the sound of *e* in the English word *egg.* The lips are parted and stretched from side to side, as if smiling. Then nasalize the **ais** sound. (See Figure 12.)

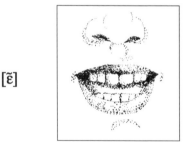

[ɛ̃]

Figure 12.
The nasal vowel sound of **in, aim, ain, im, ein**

The vowel **i,** which is always in this nasal vowel group, makes this nasal vowel sound distinctively different from the other three nasal sounds. If the vowel **i** were not in this nasal vowel combination, the nasal sound would be entirely different. It would sound more like the fourth nasal vowel sound, discussed next.

For practice, pronounce **vais,** then **vin**

> **fais,** then **fin** and **faim**
>
> **mais,** then **main**
>
> **sais,** then **sein** and **simple**

Make sure you do not pronounce the consonants **n** or **m** when pronouncing the nasal vowel groups.

Of course, there are exceptions:

[bjɛ̃]
[rjɛ̃]

bien	*well*
rien	*nothing*

These two words contain the nasal vowel combination **ien,** which is not in the same order as **ein** that was explained earlier. The nasal combination **en** in b**ien** and r**ien** normally produces a different nasal sound described as the fourth nasal vowel sound, as discussed next. Nevertheless, **ien** in b**ien** and r**ien** is pronounced the same as the other words in this third nasal vowel sound group. In the south of France you will hear b**ien** and r**ien** pronounced as in the fourth nasal vowel sound group because of the **en.**

Two other exceptions are these:

[lə sitwaˊjɛ̃]
[lɛgzaˊmɛ̃]

(le) citoy**en**	*citizen*
(l') exam**en**	*exam, examination*

In these two words, the nasal vowel combination **en** falls into the fourth nasal vowel sound, but they are pronounced like the words in this third nasal vowel sound group.

Oral Vowel Sound [ɑ]

Examples

(le) bl**â**me	*blame*
(l') **â**ge	*age*
(le) ch**â**teau	*castle*
(les) p**â**tes	*pasta*

Fourth Nasal Vowel Sound [ɑ̃]

EXAMPLES

bla**n**c	*white*
da**ns**	*in*
sa**ns**	*without*
(l') **an**ge	*angel*
(le) cha**nt**	*chant; singing*
(le) rom**an**	*novel* (literature)
(l') **am**bassade	*embassy*
(l') **am**biance	*atmosphere*
(l') **am**bula**n**ce	*ambulance*
Saint-Sa**ën**s, Camille	(French composer and organist)
(la) pe**n**te	*slope*
(la) de**nt**	*tooth*
ce**nt**	*one hundred*
(l') **em**pire	*empire*
(l') **em**ploi	*employment*
(l') ex**em**ple	*example*

Note that **en** is not nasal in the word **ennemi** *(enemy)*. It is pronounced as *en-mee.*

Review the sound of the open oral vowel **â** contained in words listed in Lesson One. You must position the lips properly to pronounce the open oral vowel **â** in those words, as you would when you say *Ah!* Then nasalize it. (See Figure 13.)

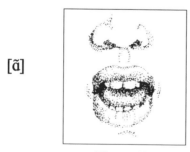

[ɑ̃]

Figure 13.
The nasal vowel sound of **an, am, en, em**

Note that the word **content** *(happy, content)* contains two different nasal sounds (**on** and **en**). However, the ending **ent** in verb forms of the third-person plural is never pronounced as a nasal sound. Compare the sound of these:

[il ɛ kɔ̃ˈtɑ̃]

Il est **cont**ent.	*He is content.*

But:

[il kɔ̃t]

Ils **cont**ent leurs malheurs. **(conter)**	*They are telling their misfortunes.*

Note also that the word **la banane** *(banana)* contains the nasal vowel spelling **an** twice. However, they are not nasalized because if you divide the word into syllables, you will see that **an** is not a nasal group: **ba-na-ne.**

Finally, to sum up the four different nasal vowel sounds in French, pronounce the following phrase that contains all four:

[œ̃ bɔ̃ vɛ̃ blɑ̃]

un bon vin blanc	*a good white wine*

Practice for Mastery

The speaker will now review all the words containing the four nasal vowels.

Note: These examples, not listed here, appeared earlier in this lesson. Just listen and repeat each word after the speaker.

Now go back to the beginning of the track and replay the review of 18 words numbered 1 to 18. This time, with a pencil, circle what you hear in each of the numbered pairs. This is a quiz on sound differentiation.

EXERCISE

1. **un**	**an**	10. **don**	**daim**
2. **bon**	**bonne**	11. **on**	**un**
3. **vent**	**vin**	12. **sans**	**saint**
4. **blond**	**blanc**	13. **nom**	**nain**
5. **vin**	**vient**	14. **dinde**	**dindon**
6. **mon**	**main**	15. **cent**	**sein**
7. **roman**	**romain**	16. **faim**	**font**
8. **bien**	**bain**	17. **ton**	**temps**
9. **vient**	**viennent**	18. **dans**	**dont**

Play the track again and check your answers before look-ing at the answers in the box.

ANSWERS

1. un	**7.** roman	**13.** nain
2. bon	**8.** bien	**14.** dindon
3. vin	**9.** vient	**15.** cent
4. blanc	**10.** daim	**16.** faim
5. vient	**11.** on	**17.** temps
6. main	**12.** sans	**18.** dans

Now pronounce aloud the two words in each group in the following list. If the nasal vowel sound is the same for both words, circle SAME. If it is not the same, circle NOT SAME.

EXERCISE

1. **cent**	**sans**	SAME	NOT SAME
2. **dans**	**dont**	SAME	NOT SAME
3. **vient**	**vent**	SAME	NOT SAME
4. **sans**	**sein**	SAME	NOT SAME
5. **vin**	**vingt**	SAME	NOT SAME
6. **chant**	**champs**	SAME	NOT SAME

7. **fin**	**faim**	SAME	NOT SAME
8. **un**	**on**	SAME	NOT SAME
9. **blanc**	**blond**	SAME	NOT SAME
10. **dent**	**dans**	SAME	NOT SAME

Now test yourself again before looking at the answers in the box below.

ANSWERS

1. SAME	**5.** SAME	**8.** NOT SAME
2. NOT SAME	**6.** SAME	**9.** NOT SAME
3. NOT SAME	**7.** SAME	**10.** SAME
4. NOT SAME		

PART TWO
THE CONSONANTS

Introducing the Sounds

Listen carefully to all the examples, repeat the French words or phrases after the speaker, then listen for the confirmation.

Most French consonants are pronounced like those in English. Consonants that are part of a single, double, or triple vowel group are pronounced differently or not at all. Refresh your memory by reviewing Lessons Three and Four in the book and on your CD.

A consonant is pronounced at the beginning of a word, within a word, next to another consonant, or before a vowel. The following two words illustrate all four positions when a consonant is normally pronounced:

EXAMPLES

[tabl]
[la fə´nɛːtr]

| (la) **table** | *table* |
| (la) **fenêtre** | *window* |

The Consonant *b*

[b]

Pronounce this consonant like the English *b*, although it is not explosive as it sometimes is in English. Note that it is pronounced as a **p** before an **s.**

Want to refresh your memory of the IPA symbols? How to read them? How to write them? How to pronounce them? Look again at pages ix–xii.

[p]

EXAMPLES

[ap´sã]
[ap´sãt]
[apsɔly´mã]

absent	*absent* (m.s.)
absente	*absent* (f.s.)
absolument	*absolutely*

The Consonant c

The consonant **c** plus **a, o, u,** or **ou** has the sound of **k.**

[k]

EXAMPLES

(le) **c**aractère	*character*
(le) **c**olis	*parcel, package*
(la) **c**uriosité	*curiosity*
(le) **c**ourage	*courage*

When **c** is before **e, i,** or **y** it has the sound of **s.**

[s]

EXAMPLES

cela	*that*
(le) **c**inéma	*cinema, movies*
(le) **c**ycle	*cycle*
Qu'est-**c**e que **c**'est que **c**ela?	*What's that?*

The Consonant ç

The consonant **ç** has the sound of **s.** The mark under the **c** is called **une cédille** *(cedilla)*. Actually, it is the lower half of the letter **s,** which tells you to pronounce it as **s.** The **ç** is used only before **a, o,** or **u** when normally **c** has the sound of **k,** as you already learned.

[s]

EXAMPLES

ça	*that* (shortening of cela)

The sound of **s** in **cela** must be retained in **ç**a:

Qu'est-ce que c'est que **ç**a?	*What's that?*
fran**ç**ais	*French*

[The sound of **s** must be retained in **français** because the word is based on **France** where **c** is pronounced **s**. If the **cédille** were not written, **c** would be pronounced **k** in front of the **a**.]

nous prononçons	*we pronounce*

[The **ç** is required here in front of **o** in order to retain the sound of **s** in the infinitive **prononcer** where **c** is pronounced **s** in front of the **e**.]

re**ç**u	*received*

[The **ç** is required here in front of **u** in order to retain the sound of **s** in the infinitive **recevoir** where **c** is pronounced **s** in front of the **e**.]

The Consonant c

This consonant is pronounced k when it is the last letter of a word.

[k]

EXAMPLES

ave**c**	*with*
(le) be**c**	*beak*
(le) ba**c**	*container; short form of le baccalau-réat,* baccalaureate degree
(le) me**c**	*guy*
(le) pi**c**	*pick, pickaxe; woodpecker*
(le) par**c**	*park*
(le) cho**c**	*shock*
(le) publi**c**	*public*
Henri de Toulouse-Lautre**c**	(French artist)
Cadilla**c**	(city in the region of Bordeaux, on the Garonne River, western France)
Honoré de Balza**c**	(French writer)

In the following words **c** is not pronounced when it is the last letter of a word.

[lə pɔːr]
[lə bɑ̃]

(le) por**c**	pork
(le) ban**c**	bench
blan**c**	white
(le) fran**c**	franc
l'estoma**c**	stomach
(le) taba**c**	tobacco

However, the final **c** is pronounced **k** in porc and épic in the following word.

[k]

[lə pɔrkeˊpik]

(le) por**c**-épi**c**	porcupine

Note, also, that the final **c** of a masculine singular adjective changes to **que** in the feminine form because the **k** sound must be retained.

EXAMPLES

[lɛnˊmi pyˊblik]
[la vɑ̃ ːt pyˊblik]

(l') ennemi publi**c**	public enemy
(la) vente publi**que**	public sale

Finally, note that **c** in these words has a hard **g** sound as in the English word *go*.

[g]

[səˊgɔ̃]
[səˊgɔ̃d]

se**c**ond	second (m.s.)
se**c**onde	second (f.s.)
se**c**ondaire	secondary

The Consonants *cc*

Pronounce **cc** as **k** when followed by **a, o, u,** or **ou.**

[k]

EXAMPLES

[akɑˊble]

	ac**c**abler	*to overwhelm*
(l')	ac**c**ord	*agreement*
	ac**c**user	*to accuse*
	ac**c**ourir	*to rush up, to run up to*

Pronounce **cc** as **ks** when followed by **e** or **i.**

[ks]

EXAMPLES

[lakˊsɛ]

	ac**c**epter	*to accept*
(l')	ac**c**ès	*access*
(l')	ac**c**ident	*accident*

The Consonants *ch*

The consonants **ch** plus a vowel are generally pronounced *sh* as in the English word *shop.*

[ʃ]

EXAMPLES

[lə ʃa]

[la ʃyt]

[lə ʃuˊflœːr]

(le)	**ch**at	*cat*
(le)	**ch**eval	*horse*
(la)	**ch**imie	*chemistry*
(le)	**ch**ocolat	*chocolate*
(la)	**ch**ute	*fall*
(le)	para**ch**ute	*parachute*
(le)	**ch**ou	*cabbage*
(le)	**ch**ou-fleur	*cauliflower*

In the following words **ch** has the sound of **k** in front of a vowel because they are derived from the Greek language and the sound of **k** is retained:

[k]

[lə ka´o]

(le) **ch**aos	*chaos*
(l') é**ch**o	*echo*
(la) **ch**orégraphie	*choreography*
(le) **ch**oeur	*chorus, choir*
(l') or**ch**estre	*orchestra*

[lɔr´kɛstr]

The Consonant *d*

[d]

Pronounce **d** like the English **d**. It is generally not pronounced when at the end of a word.

Examples

[lə bɔːr]
[lə nɔːr]

(le) bor**d**	*edge*
(le) nor**d**	*north*

The final **d** is pronounced in this word:

[lə syd]

(le) su**d**	*south*

Review Lessons Three and Four where **d** appears in combinations with vowels, such as **aud, id, ied,** and others.

When a word ends in **d** it is pronounced as **t,** connecting it with the word after it if that word begins with a vowel or silent **h:**

[t]

EXAMPLES

[œ̃ grɑ̃ taˈmuːr]

un gran**d** amour	*a great love*
un gran**d** homme	*a great man*
Quan**d** elle parle,	*When she talks,*
	(parler)
elle me fait rire.	*she makes me*
	laugh.
	(faire rire)

Practice for Mastery

The speaker will now review all the words containing consonants in the preceding section.

Note: These examples, not listed here, appeared earlier in this lesson. Just listen and repeat each word after the speaker.

Now pronounce aloud the words in the following list. If the consonant c is pronounced like the sound of **s,** circle LIKE S. If **c** is pronounced like the sound of **k,** circle LIKE K.

EXERCISE

1.	**le colis**	LIKE S	LIKE K
2.	**cela**	LIKE S	LIKE K
3.	**ça**	LIKE S	LIKE K
4.	**le cinéma**	LIKE S	LIKE K
5.	**nous prononçons**	LIKE S	LIKE K
6.	**recevoir**	LIKE S	LIKE K
7.	**le garçon**	LIKE S	LIKE K
8.	**le curé**	LIKE S	LIKE K
9.	**le cas**	LIKE S	LIKE K
10.	**le cou**	LIKE S	LIKE K

Test yourself again before looking at the answers in the box.

ANSWERS

1. LIKE K	3. LIKE S	5. LIKE S	7. LIKE S	9. LIKE K
2. LIKE S	4. LIKE S	6. LIKE S	8. LIKE K	10. LIKE K

Now pronounce aloud the words in this list. If the final **c** is pronounced like **k,** circle YES. If it is not pronounced at all, circle NO.

EXERCISE

1. **avec**	YES	NO	4. **le parc**	YES	NO
2. **le porc**	YES	NO	5. **le banc**	YES	NO
3. **le pic**	YES	NO	6. **le bec**	YES	NO

Test yourself again before looking at the answers in the box.

ANSWERS

1. YES	2. NO	3. YES	4. YES	5. NO	6. YES

Finally, pronounce aloud the words in this list. If **ch** is pronounced like **sh,** circle **sh.** If like **k,** circle **k.**

EXERCISE

1. **le chat**	sh	k	4. **la chanson**	sh	k
2. **le chaos**	sh	k	5. **le choeur**	sh	k
3. **le chocolat**	sh	k	6. **le chou**	sh	k

Test yourself again before looking at the answers in the box.

ANSWERS

1. sh	2. k	3. sh	4. sh	5. k	6. sh

Here's some sound advice: Listen to the pronunciation CD for a few minutes every day!

Introducing the Sounds

Listen carefully to all the examples, repeat the French words or phrases after the speaker, then listen for the confirmation.

The Consonant *f*

The consonant **f** is generally pronounced in any position of a word.

[f]

EXAMPLES

	(la) **f**oi	*faith*
	neu**f**	*nine*
	(le) veu**f**	*widower*
	informati**f**	*informative*
[lœf]	(l') oeu**f**	*egg*
[lə bœf]	(le) boeu**f**	*ox, beef*
	(la) soi**f**	*thirst*
[lə ʃɛf]	(le) che**f**	*chief, boss*

Do not pronounce the **f** in **(la) clef**/*key*. It sounds like *clay*. Note that it is also spelled **clé**.

Do not pronounce the **f** in the following words:

[lə ʃɛˊdœːvr]	(le) che**f**-d'oeuvre	*masterpiece*
[le zø]	(les) oeu**f**s	*eggs*
[le bø]	(les) boeu**f**s	*oxen; beef* (pl.)
	[Review the clusters **oeuf** and **oeuvre** under the vowel **o** in Lesson Three.]	

When the word **neuf** is followed by a word beginning with a vowel or silent **h,** the **f** is pronounced like a **v.**

[nœ´vã]	neuf ans	nine years
[il ɛ nœ´vœːr]	Il est neuf heures.	It is nine o'clock.
	(être)	

The Consonant *g*

Pronounce **g** + **a, o** or **u** like *g* in the English words *game, go, gum.*

EXAMPLES

[lə gã]	(le) **g**ant	glove
[la gɔm]	(la) **g**omme	rubber eraser
[la gɛːr]	(la) **g**uerre	war
	(la) **g**ueule	mouth (of an animal)
	guère	hardly, scarcely

Pronounce **g** + **e, i** or **y** like *s* in the English words *measure* and *leisure,* or like the *z* in *seizure.* Do not pronounce it *dg* as in the English word *fudge.*

EXAMPLES

[lə ʒə´ã]	(le) **g**éant	giant
	rou**ge**	red
	(le) **g**ilet	vest
	(la) **g**ymnastique	gymnastics
[ʒɔrʒ]	**Ge**or**ge**s Bizet	(French composer)
	André **G**i**d**e	(French writer)
	Gigi	(girl's nickname for **Ge**or**ge**tte)

The Consonants *gn*

This is pronounced like *ni* in the English word *onion* or like *ny* in the English word *canyon.*

[ɲ]

EXAMPLES

[lɔ'ɲɔ̃]

(l') oi**gn**on	*onion*
(la) monta**gn**e	*mountain*
(le) si**gn**al	*signal*
Alfred de Vi**gn**y	(French poet)

[vi'ɲi]

But pronounce hard g + n, as in the English word *diagnostic*, French word, **diagnostique**.

The Consonant *h*

The consonant **h** is never pronounced.

EXAMPLES

[lɔpi'tal]

(l') **h**ôpital	*hospital*
(l') **h**ospitalité	*hospitality*
(l') **h**ôte	*host*
(l') **h**ôtesse	*hostess*
(l') **h**ôtel	*hotel*

[lo'tɛl]

The letter **h** is aspirate in the following words. This means that it is treated like a consonant, so there is no liaison or elision. Do not pronounce **h** in French even though it is designated as aspirate.

[ɔːr də]

hors de	*out of, outside of*
hors d'ici!	*get out of here!*
hors d'usage	*unserviceable, out of order*
de**h**ors	*outside*
au-de**h**ors	*on the outside*
(les) **h**ors-d'oeuvre	*hors-d'oeuvre*
Les Halles	(a famous market in Paris)

[le ɔr'dœvr]
[le al]

Nouns beginning with the aspirate **h** require the definite article **le** or **la** rather than **l'** in front of them:

EXAMPLES

[lə ɑːvr]
[lə ɑːvr]

[lə ariˊko vɛːr]

le havre	*harbor, port*
Le Havre	(French seaport in northern France on the English Channel)
le haut	*top*
la hauteur	*height*
le haricot vert	*green string bean*

A word beginning with aspirate **h** is designated as ***h** or **'h** or **•h** in a French dictionary. A liaison is never made with a word beginning with aspirate **h.** And no elision is made; in other words, it is not correct to use l' or d' in front of a word beginning with aspirate h. Note: **le havre, de hauteur.** See **La Liaison** in Lesson Nine. See also **élision** in Lesson Ten.

The Consonant *j*

Pronounce **j** like the *s* in the English words *measure* and *leisure,* or like the *z* in *seizure.*

[ʒ]

EXAMPLES

[ʒə]

[ʒɔˊli]

je	*I*
Jean	*John*
Jeanne	*Jean, Jane, Joan*
jouer	*to play*
je joue	*I play, I am playing* **(jouer)**
(le) **j**ouet	*toy*
joli, **j**olie	*pretty*

The Consonant *l*

[1]

The consonant **l** is pronounced properly when the tip of the tongue is placed lightly against the inside of the two upper front teeth. In English, however, we tend to pronounce the consonant **l** way back in the mouth with the tip of the tongue touching the palate, the roof of the mouth.

EXAMPLES

[li´li]
[lə lis]

	Lily	*Lily* (proper name)
	(le) lis, lys	*lily* (flower)
	il lit	*he is reading* (**lire**)
	(le) lit	*bed*
	(le) livre	*book*
	(le) sel	*salt*
	final	*final*

The Consonants *ll*

[1]

Double **ll** is usually pronounced like the single **l.**

EXAMPLES

[ɛl]
[bɛl]

[la sal]
[la sɛl]

	elle	*she; her*
	belle	*beautiful* (f.s.)
	(la) ville	*city*
	(le) bulletin	*bulletin*
	mille	*one thousand*
	(la) salle	*large room*
	(la) selle	*saddle*

When **l** or **ll** is in a cluster with vowels, the sound of *y* is produced, as in the English words *yes* and *yellow*. Review the clusters **ail, aille, aillent, eil, eils, eille, eilles, euil, euils, euille, euilles, ille, illes,** and others, in Lesson Three. Remember that the **l** is pronounced in **aile** (f.s.) / *wing*.

The Consonants *m, n*

[m] [n]

These two consonants are pronounced as in English. However, at times, the vowel in front of them *in the same syllable* is nasalized, as in bo**n,** mo**n,** no**n,** no**m,** bo**m**be, i**m**portant, in which case the **m** and **n** are not pronounced. Review **The Four Nasal Vowels** in Lesson Five.

The Consonant *p*

[p]

This consonant is not explosive like the English *p* when pronounced.

EXAMPLES

[pa′pa]

[puːr]

(le) **pa**pa	*dad, pop*	
payer	*to pay*	
(la) **pi**pe	*pipe*	
parce que	*because*	
pour	*for*	

Do not pronounce **p** when it is the last letter of a French word.

EXAMPLES

[ləku]
[bo′ku]
[tro]

(le) cou**p**	*hit, blow*	
beaucou**p**	*much, many, a lot*	
tro**p**	*too much, too many*	

But do pronounce **p** in this expression:

[a′le ɔp]

Allez, ho**p**!	*Hop to it!* (an interjection to express an abrupt action) **(aller)**

The final **p** is pronounced in English words used in the French language.

EXAMPLES

[lə bɔp]

(le) bo**p**	bop
(le) be-bo**p**	bebop
sto**p**	stop
(la) musique po**p**	pop music
(le) ra**p**	rap music

[la myˊzik pɔp]
[lə rap]

Do not pronounce **p** in these words:

[ʒə rɔ̃]
[lə kɔ̃ːt]

je rom**ps**	to break, shatter
(le) com**pte**	account
com**pter**	to count
(la) com**ptabilité**	accounting
dom**pter**	to tame
(le) dom**pteur**	tamer (m.s.)
(la) dom**pteuse**	tamer (f.s.)
(le) cor**ps**	body

[lə kɔːr]

In this word, **p** is not pronounced but **t** is:

[sɛt]

se**pt**	seven

But in this word, both **p** and **t** are pronounced:

[sɛpˊtɑ̃ːbr]

se**pt**embre	September

The Consonants *ph*

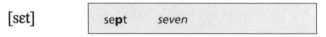

The French consonants **ph** are pronounced like the English *ph*.

EXAMPLES

[fi´lip]

	Philippe	*Philip*
(la)	**ph**oto	*photo*
(la)	**ph**otogra**ph**ie	*photography*

[la fɔtɔgra´fi]

The Consonants *ps*

[ps]

At the beginning of a word **ps** is pronounced *ps.*

EXAMPLES

[la psikɔlɔ´ʒi]

(la)	**ps**ychologie	*psychology*
	psychologique	*psychological*
(la)	**ps**ychiatrie	*psychiatry*

[la psikja´tri]

The Consonant *q + u*

[k]

The combination **q** + **u** produces the sound of **k.**

EXAMPLES

[ki]

qui	*who*
Qui est là?	*Who is there?* **(être)**
Qui est-ce **qu**i a fait cela?	*Who is it who did that?*
Que dites-vous?	*What are you saying?*
Qui répondra à la **qu**estion **qu**e j'ai posée?	*Who will reply to the question I asked?*
Quelle **qu**estion!	*What a question!*
Québec	*(francophone province in Canada)*

[kɛl kɛs´tjɔ̃]

The Consonant *r*

[r]

There are three ways to pronounce the **r** in French, but we concentrate on the Parisian **r** that you hear on your CD. It is also known as the dorsal **r** because it is articulated with the dorsum (outer surface) of the tongue. Press the tip of the tongue gently against the lower front teeth. Raise the tongue toward the soft palate and let the air from your throat softly vibrate the uvula, as if you are about to gargle (see Figure 14).

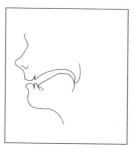

Figure 14.
The consonant **r**

Examples

[lə re´zɛ̃]

	(le) **raisin**	*grape*
	(la) **raison**	*reason*
	(la) **rue**	*street*
	(le) **cor de chasse**	*hunting horn*
	(le) **cor d'harmonie**	*French horn*
[lə kɔːr]	(le) **corps**	*body*
	(la) **fleur**	*flower*
[lə kœːr]	(le) **coeur**	*heart*

Review the pronunciation of infinitives ending in **er** and words ending in **er** or **ère** under those combinations in Lesson Three.

The Consonant s

[s]

The consonant **s** is pronounced like the English *s* in *sit*.

EXAMPLES

[syr]
[lə swaːr]

sur	*on*
(le) **s**oir	*evening*

The final **s** in a word is not pronounced.

EXAMPLES

[le pɔm]

[me sœːr]

(les) pomme**s**	*apples*
(les) femme**s**	*women*
(les) livre**s**	*books*
mes soeur**s**	*my sisters*

For words that contain a final **s** that is pronounced, review Lesson Three.

When a single **s** is preceded and followed by a vowel, it sounds like a **z.**

[z]

EXAMPLES

[pwaˊzɔ̃]

[kuˊzɛ̃]
[kuˊzin]

(le) poi**s**on	*poison*
(la) ro**s**e	*rose*
(le) dé**s**ert	*desert*
(la) ru**s**e	*ruse, trick*
(le) cou**s**in	*cousin (m.s.)*
(la) cou**s**ine	*cousin (f.s.)*
Françoi**s**e Sagan	*(French author)*

The Consonants *ss*

[s]

The double consonants **ss** are pronounced like *ss* in the English word *possible*.

EXAMPLES

[pɔ´siblə]	po**ss**ible	*possible*
	(le) ma**ss**age	*massage*
	(le) me**ss**age	*message*
[lə pwa´sɔ̃]	(le) poi**ss**on	*fish*
	(le) de**ss**ert	*dessert*
	ru**ss**e	*Russian*
[lə ku´sɛ̃]	(le) cou**ss**in	*cushion*
[klod dəby´si]	Claude Debu**ss**y	(French composer)

Practice for Mastery

The speaker will now review all the words containing consonants in the preceding section.

Note: These examples, not listed here, appeared earlier in this lesson. Just listen and repeat each word after the speaker.

Now go back to the beginning of the track and replay the review of six groups of words numbered 1 to 6. This time, with a pencil, circle what you hear in each of the numbered pairs. This is a quiz on sound differentiation.

EXERCISE

1. **poisson**	poison		4. **désert**	dessert
2. **François**	Françoise		5. **russe**	ruse
3. **cousin**	coussin		6. **lise**	lisse

Play the track again and check your answers before looking at the answers in the box.

ANSWERS

1. poisson	**3.** coussin	**5.** russe
2. Françoise	**4.** désert	**6.** lise

Now pronounce aloud the words in the following list. If the consonant **g** is pronounced like the hard *g* in the English word *go*, circle A. If the **g** is pronounced like *s* in the English words *measure, leisure,* and *occasion,* circle B.

EXERCISE

1. **le gant**	A	B	4. **André Gide**	A	B
2. **le géant**	A	B	5. **la gomme**	A	B
3. **le gilet**	A	B	6. **le guide**	A	B

Test yourself again before looking at the answers in the box.

ANSWERS

1. A	**2.** B	**3.** B	**4.** B	**5.** A	**6.** A

Pronounce aloud the words in the following list. If the consonant **p** is pronounced, circle YES. If it is not pronounced, circle NO.

EXERCISE

1. **le coup**	YES	NO	4. **compter**	YES	NO
2. **la coupe**	YES	NO	5. **allez, hop!**	YES	NO
3. **beaucoup**	YES	NO	6. **trop**	YES	NO

Test yourself again before looking at the answers in the box.

ANSWERS

1. NO	**2.** YES	**3.** NO	**4.** NO	**5.** YES	**6.** NO

Pronounce aloud the words in this list. If the consonant **r** is pronounced, circle YES. If it is not pronounced, circle NO.

EXERCISE

1. **hier**	YES NO		4. **la rue**	YES NO	
2. **aller**	YES NO		5. **donner**	YES NO	
3. **cher**	YES NO		6. **l'hiver**	YES NO	

Test yourself again before looking at the answers in the box.

ANSWERS

> **1.** YES **2.** NO **3.** YES **4.** YES **5.** NO **6.** YES

Practice in Context

Now listen to the speakers pronounce four statements drilling certain consonant sounds. During the pauses, repeat each sentence after the speaker imitating the intonation, rise and fall of the voice, and rhythm.

Lily lit le livre dans le lit.

Lily is reading the book in bed.

Papa, as-tu payé beaucoup pour ta pipe?

Dad, did you pay a lot for your pipe?

Vois-tu le ver vert qui va vers le verre vert?

Do you see the green worm going toward the green glass?

Le chasseur, sachant chasser sans son chien, chassera seul.

The hunter, knowing how to hunt without his dog, will hunt alone.

---

coupon [ku´pɔ̃] is often pronounced "kewpon" in English. Remember, do you drive a *coupe* or a *cupe*?

Introducing the Sounds

Listen carefully to all the examples, repeat the French words or phrases after the speaker, then listen for the confirmation.

The Consonant *t*

[t]

The French consonant **t** is pronounced like the English *t*.

EXAMPLES

[lə ty´ty]

	(le) **tut**u	tutu, ballet skirt
	tris**t**e	sad
	(la) **t**ris**t**esse	sadness
[tytɛ´ty]	**Tu t'**es **t**u.	You kept silent.
		(se taire)

Normally, **t** is not pronounced when it is the last letter of a word:

[pə´ti]

	peti**t**	small, little
[lə re´si]	(l') appéti**t**	appetite
[il fi´ni]	(le) réci**t**	recitation
	Il (Elle) fini**t**.	He (She) finishes.
		(finir)

When a word is of one syllable, the **t** is sometimes pronounced:

[la dɔt]

(la)	do**t**	dowry
	ce**t**	this
	ne**t**	clean, neat, tidy
(le)	Ne**t**	Internet

[sɛt]

	sep**t**	seven
	hui**t**	eight

[zyt]

	Zu**t**!	Oh, shoot!

Do not pronounce the **t** in these words of one syllable:

[e]
[il ɛ, ɛl ɛ]
[il di, ɛl di]

e**t**	and
Il (Elle) es**t**.	He (She) is. (**être**)
Il (Elle) di**t**.	He (She) says. (**dire**)

Review in Lesson Three words ending in **ect** as well as these words where the final **t** is pronounced:

[ɛst]
[wɛst]

es**t**	east
oues**t**	west
correc**t**	correct

Pronounce the **t** like **s** in these word endings: **-tion, -tial, -tiel, -tie, -tieux, -tieuse.**

[s]

[la prɔnɔ̃sja´sjɔ̃]

(la)	prononcia**t**ion	pronunciation
(l')	ini**t**ial	initial
	par**t**iel	partial

[la demɔkra´si]

(la)	démocra**t**ie	democracy
	supersti**t**ieux	superstitious

[ɑ̃bi´sjøz]

ambi**t**ieuse	ambitious

The Consonants *th*

[t]

The combination **th** is pronounced like the English *t*. In the French language, there is no *th* sound as in the English words *thin* or *this*.

EXAMPLES

[lə te]

[la kate´dral]

[teɔ´dɔr]

[nata´li]

(le)	**th**é	*tea*
(le)	**th**éâtre	*theater*
(la)	**th**éorie	*theory*
(le)	**th**ème	*theme*
(la)	ca**th**édrale	*cathedral*
(l')	a**th**lète	*athlete*
(la)	mé**th**ode	*method*
	Théodore	*Theodore*
	Na**th**an	*Nathan*
	Na**th**alie	*Nathalie, Natalie*
	Na**th**aniel	*Nathaniel*

The Consonant *v*

[v]

The French consonant **v** is pronounced like the English *v*.

EXAMPLES

[vi´vjɛn]

[lə vãdrə´di]

	Vivienne	*Vivian, Vivienne*
	il (elle) **v**eut	*he (she) wants*
		(vouloir)
(la)	**v**iande	*meat*
	a**v**ant	*before*
(le)	**v**endredi	*Friday*

The Consonant *w*

[w]

Pronounce the French consonant **w** like the English *w* in words borrowed from the English language.

EXAMPLES

[lə wik´ɛnd]

(le) **w**eek-end	*weekend*
(le) **w**hisky	*whisky*
(le) **w**estern	*western*

In some French words, the **w** is pronounced **v.**

[v]

EXAMPLES

[lə va´gõ restɔ´rã]

(le) **w**agon-restaurant	*dining car* (on a train)
(le) **w**agon-couchettes	*sleeping car* (on a train)
(les) **W**C	*water closet, toilet*
[Pronounce **WC** as *vay-say* or *doo-ble vay-say*.]	

The Consonant *x*

[ks]

The consonant **x** is pronounced *ks* when a consonant follows it.

EXAMPLES

[ɛksɛ´lã]

e**x**cellent	*excellent*
(l') e**x**pertise	*expertise*
(l') e**x**tase	*ecstasy*
e**x**travagant	*extravagant*

Pronounce **x** like *gz* when a vowel precedes and follows it.

[gz]

EXAMPLES

[εgza´mɛ̃]

(l') e**x**amen	*exam, examination*
(l') e**x**emple	*example*
(l') e**x**ercice	*exercise*
e**x**ister	*to exist*

When **x** is the last letter of a word, it is not pronounced.

EXAMPLES

[œ´rø]

heureu**x**	*happy*
(les) cheveu**x**	*hair*
(les) chevau**x**	*horses*
deu**x**	*two*
beau**x**	*handsome, beautiful*

Review in Lesson Three the combination **aix** when **x** is pronounced. Note that the final **x** in **le phénix**/*phoenix* is pronounced.

Pronounce **x** like **z** when there is a vowel after it.

[z]

EXAMPLES

[dø´zjɛm]

[le bo´zar]

deu**x**ième	*second* (of more than two)
(les) beau**x**-arts	*the fine arts*

When **x** is the first letter of a word plus vowel, it is pronounced *ks*.

[ks]

EXAMPLES

[la ksenɔfɔˊbi]

(la) **x**énophobie	*xenophobia*
(le) **x**ylophone	*xylophone*
(la) **x**érographie	*xerography*

When referring to an unknown person as **X,** pronounce **x** as *eeks,* which is the word for the letter **x** of the French alphabet.

[iks]

EXAMPLES

[maˊdam iks]
[məˊsjø iks]

Madame **X**	*Madam X*
Monsieur **X**	*Mister X*

The Consonant *z*

[z]

The French consonant **z** is pronounced like the English *z*.

EXAMPLES

[lə zeˊro]

[zɛ̃ˊzɛ̃]

[zyt]

(le) **z**éro	*zero*
(le) **z**èbre	*zebra*
zin**z**in	*crazy*
(le) **z**oo	*zoo*
Zut!	*Oh shoot!*

Do not pronounce the **z** in words ending in **ez.**

EXAMPLES

[a ˊse]

[ʃe]

[prɔnɔ̃ ˊse]

	asse**z**	*enough*
(le)	ne**z**	*nose*
	che**z**	*at the place* (home) *of*
	Parle**z**!	*Speak!* (**parler**)
	Prononce**z**!	*Pronounce!* (**prononcer**)

Review the combination **ez** in Lesson Three.

Practice for Mastery

The speaker will now review words containing consonants in the preceding section.

Note: These examples, which are not listed here, appeared earlier in this lesson. Just listen and repeat each word after the speaker.

Pronounce aloud the words in the following list. If the **t** at the end of the word is pronounced, circle YES. If it is not pronounced, circle NO.

Exercise

1. **sept**	YES	NO	5. **instant**	YES	NO	
2. **et**	YES	NO	6. **petit**	YES	NO	
3. **net**	YES	NO	7. **huit**	YES	NO	
4. **il est**	YES	NO	8. **il finit**	YES	NO	

Test yourself again before looking at the answers in the box.

Answers

1. YES	**3.** YES	**5.** NO	**7.** YES
2. NO	**4.** NO	**6.** NO	**8.** NO

Pronounce aloud the words in this list. If the **t** is pronounced as **t**, circle **T.** If it is pronounced as **s,** circle **S.**

Exercise

1. **partiel**	T	S	4. **minutieuse**	T	S
2. **l'initial**	T	S	5. **prononciation**	T	S
3. **ambitieux**	T	S	6. **la démocratie**	T	S

Answers

The consonant **t** in all these words is pronounced as **s.**

Pronounce aloud the words in this list. If **w** is pronounced like the English *w*, circle **W.** If it is pronounced like the English *v*, circle **V.**

EXERCISE

1. **le week-end**	W	V	4. **le wagon-restaurant**	W	V
2. **le wagon**	W	V	5. **les WC**	W	V
3. **le western**	W	V	6. **le wagon-couchettes**	W	V

ANSWERS

1. W	**2.** V	**3.** W	**4.** V	**5.** V	**6.** V

Finally, pronounce aloud the words in this list. If **x** is pronounced *ks*, circle *ks*. If it is pronounced *gz*, circle *gz*.

EXERCISE

1. **excellent**	*ks*	*gz*	4. **l'examen**	*ks*	*gz*
2. **l'exercice**	*ks*	*gz*	5. **expert**	*ks*	*gz*
3. **le xylophone**	*ks*	*gz*	6. **la xérographie**	*ks*	*gz*

ANSWERS

1. *ks*	2. *gz*	3. *ks*	4. *gz*	5. *ks*	6. *ks*

How are you doing on these tests? Good idea to test yourself again so you can pronounce them perfectly. Like the speakers on your CD!

PART THREE
WORD PATTERNS
AND INTONATION

Introducing the Sounds

Listen carefully to all the examples and repeat the French words or phrases after the speaker.

When a word ends in a consonant that is normally *not* pronounced, a liaison is made by pronouncing the consonant if the word that follows begins with a vowel or silent h.

Les enfants sont allés à l'école sans argent.

[le zã´fã sɔ̃ ta´le a le´kɔl sã zar´ʒã]

The children went to school without money.

In making the liaison, the pronounced consonant becomes part of the syllable at the beginning of the word that follows. If the consonant is **s**, it is pronounced as **z.** In other words, in the example here, when pronouncing **s** in **les** as **z,** the sound goes with **en** in **enfants. Les** is still pronounced as *lay*, but the **z** sound of **s** in **les** is pronounced *with* the word **enfants** so it sounds like this:

lay zenfants **[le zã´fã]**

A liaison is not always made whenever a word ends in a consonant and the word that follows begins with a vowel or silent *h*. There are times when a liaison is required, when it is recommended, and when it is prohibited.

Required liaison

Between a personal subject pronoun and the verb:

EXAMPLES

[nu za´lɔ̃]	**nous allons**	*we are going* **(aller)**
	vous êtes	*you are* **(être)**
	ils ont	*they have* **(avoir)**
	elles iront	*they will go* **(aller)**
[ɔ̃ na´pɛl]	**on appelle**	*someone is calling*
		(appeler)

Between a preceding personal pronoun when it is the direct or indirect object of the verb:

[il nu za´pɛl]	**Il nous appelle.**	*He is calling us.*
		(appeler)
[ɛl vu za´nɔ̃ːs]	**Elle vous annonce**	*She is announcing*
	les nouvelles.	*the news to you.*
		(annoncer)

Between a preceding direct object pronoun referring to persons or things and the verb:

[ʒə le´zɛm]	**Je les aime.**	*I like them.* **(aimer)**

Between a determinant (for example, **les, des, aux, ces**) or an adjective (for example, **grands, petits, tout, deux, mes, nos, vos, leurs**) and the noun or adjective:

[le zety´djã]	**les étudiants**	*the students*
	des amis	*some friends*
	aux églises	*to (at) the churches*
		[Note that **x** is pronounced as **z** when making a liaison.]

[le grɑ̃ˊzum]	ces arbres	*these trees*
[de pəˊti zɑ̃ˊfɑ̃]	les grands hommes	*the great men*
	des petits enfants	*little children*
	de tout âge	*of all ages*
	deux accidents	*two accidents*
	mes amis	*my friends*
	nos ancêtres	*our ancestors*
	vos affaires	*your business (affairs)*
[lœr zɑ̃ˊsjɛ̃ zeˊlɛv]	leurs anciens élèves	*their former pupils*

With the pronoun **en** (of them, some of them):

[ʒɑ̃ ne dø]	J'en ai deux.	*I have two of them.* **(avoir)**
	Prenez-en.	*Take some.* **(prendre)**
[alevu ˊzɑ̃]	Allez-vous-en!	*Go away!* **(s'en aller)**

With the pronoun **y** (there, to it, in it):

[ale ˊzi]	Allez-y.	*Go there (Go to it).* **(aller)**
[ilzi ˊsɔ̃]	Ils y sont.	*They are there.* **(être)**

With the inverted subject and verb in the interrogative:

[kədi ´tɛl]

Que dit-elle?	*What is she saying?*
	(dire)
Que prend-il?	*What is he taking?*
	(prendre)
[Here, **d** is pronounced as **t**. Review the consonant **d** in Lesson Six, The Consonants: I.]	
Que dirait-on?	*What would one say?*
	(dire)
Viennent-ils?	*Are they coming?*
	(venir)

[vjɛn ´til]

After a preposition of one syllable:

[dã ´zœ̃ nɛ̃s´tã]

dans un instant	*in an instant*
sous un parapluie	*under an umbrella*
en Angleterre	*to (in) England*
sans argent	*without any money*
chez elle	*at her house*

[ʃe ´zɛl]

With adverbs of one syllable and adverbs of negation:

[pɑzã´kɔr]

pas encore	*not yet*
ne jamais appeler	*never to call*
plus important	*more important*
moins aimable	*less likable*
bien assez	*quite enough*
assez étroit	*rather narrow*
trop amoureux	*too much in love*
de plus en plus	*more and more*
très intéressant	*very interesting*

[trɛzɛ̃tere´sã]

With impersonal **il est** or **c'est**:

[ilɛtɛ̃pɔ´siblə]

Il est impossible.	*It is impossible.*
	(être)
C'est étrange.	*It's strange.*
	(être)

[sɛtе´trãːʒ]

With many locutions (a group of words) or compound words:

[də tãzã ´tã]

de temps en temps	*from time to time*
mot à mot	*word by word*
aux États-Unis	*to (in) the United States*
vis-à-vis	*face to face*
de mieux en mieux	*better and better*

[də mjøzã ´mjø]

Recommended liaison

With **quand** and **dont**:

EXAMPLES

[kãtɔ̃ ´parl]

Quand on parle . . .	*When one is speaking. . .*
	(parler)
dont il a besoin	*of which he has need*
	(avoir)

Between the verb and a noun or complementary adjective:

[nusɔmza´mi]

Nous	*We are friends*
sommes⁀amis.	**(être)**
Elles	*They are happy.*
sont⁀heureuses.	**(être)**

Between the helping verb in the third-person singular or plural and the past participle in a compound tense:

[ɛlɛtari´ve]

Elle est⁀arrivée.	*She has arrived.*
	(être, arriver)
Ils⁀avaient⁀été	*They had been here.*
ici.	**(avoir, être)**

Prohibited liaison

A liaison is not made (when normally it would be) if there is a significant pause between both elements while speaking:

Elle est .... heureuse.	*She is .... happy.*

With the conjunction **et:**

lui et elle	*he and she*

With the final consonant of a noun in the singular:

un nez énorme	*an enormous nose*

With the **-es** ending of a verb in the second-person singular, present indicative and present subjunctive:

Tu parles	*You speak*
admirablement.	*admirably.* **(parler)**

If the word that follows begins with an aspirate **h:**

> **des hors-d'oeuvre**   *some hors d'oeuvres*
> **les haricots verts**   *green string beans*
> [Review the aspirate **h** under the consonant **h** in Lesson Seven, Consonants: II.]

Practice for Mastery

The speaker will now review words, phrases, and sentences in the preceding section.

Note: These examples, which are not listed here, appeared earlier in this unit. Just listen and repeat after the speaker during the pauses, paying careful attention to liaisons that are made or not made.

Now pronounce aloud the phrases in the following list numbered 1 to 14. If a liaison is made, circle YES. If a liaison is not made, circle NO.

EXERCISE

1. **nous allons**	YES	NO	8. **les haricots**	YES	NO
2. **vous êtes**	YES	NO	9. **ils y sont**	YES	NO
3. **ils ont**	YES	NO	10. **elle est allée**	YES	NO
4. **nous avons**	YES	NO	11. **Que dit-il?**	YES	NO
5. **lui et elle**	YES	NO	12. **les hors-d'oeuvre**	YES	NO
6. **États-Unis**	YES	NO	13. **Allez-y!**	YES	NO
7. **Tu parles assez.**	YES	NO	14. **un nez énorme**	YES	NO

Test yourself again before looking at the answers in the box.

ANSWERS

1. YES	**4.** YES	**7.** NO	**10.** YES	**13.** YES
2. YES	**5.** NO	**8.** NO	**11.** YES	**14.** NO
3. YES	**6.** YES	**9.** YES	**12.** NO	

Practice in Context

Now listen to a short narration in which several liaisons are made. During the pauses, repeat each sentence or phrase after the speaker imitating the intonation, rise and fall of the voice, and rhythm.

Nous avons des amis qui sont allés aux États-Unis. Ils ont laissé leurs deux enfants chez nous. Aujourd'hui mon mari et moi nous allons avec leurs enfants nous amuser et accueillir les oiseaux dans un parc.

We have some friends who went to the United States. They left their two children at our house. Today my husband and I are going with their children to have fun and welcome the birds in a park.

Introducing the Sounds

Listen carefully to all the examples and repeat the French words or phrases after the speaker.

L'Enchaînement

When a word ends in a consonant that is normally pronounced, an **enchaînement** is made by linking the consonant to form a syllable with the word that follows if it begins with a vowel or silent **h.**

EXAMPLE

[lamu rar´dã]

| **l'amour ardent** | *ardent love* |

The consonant **r** in **amour** is always pronounced. The word that follows begins with a vowel. In this group, pronounce the **r** in **amour** not as part of the word **amour,** but rather with the **a** in **ardent.** It sounds like this: *amou-rardent.*

L'Élision

An **élision** *(elision)* is made when the final **e** or **a** of a word is omitted and an apostrophe is added, if the word that follows begins with a vowel or silent **h.** In doing so, a syllable is formed with the beginning of the word that follows. The most commonly used words that make up an **élision** are **le, la, je, me, te, se, de, ce, ne, que,** and words ending in **que.**

Don't forget that the mark ´ indicates that the stress falls on the syllable after it. Note also that the mark : indicates the vowel sound in front of it is long. Reminder: The mark ~ over a vowel means it is nasal, as in *bon* [bõ].

Examples

[la′mi dan]

l'ami d'Anne	Anne's friend (m.)
l'amie d'Albert	Albert's friend (f.)
l'ennemi	the enemy
l'homme	the man
l'hôtel	the hotel
j'ai	I have (avoir)
Je l'ai.	I have it.
Je m'appelle Jean.	My name is John.

[sɛ vrɛ]

C'est vrai.	It's true. (être)
Ce n'est pas vrai.	It's not true.
Je t'écoute.	I'm listening to you. (écouter)
d'après	according to
Je n'ai pas assez d'argent.	I don't have enough money. (avoir)
Qu'est-ce qu'il dit?	What is he saying? (dire)
lorsqu'elle était jeune . . .	when she was young . . . (être)

[ʒyska də′mɛ̃]

jusqu'à demain	until tomorrow

Exceptions: First of all, do not assume an elision is made with all words that end in **e** or **a.** Study the most common ones in the list here.

- Do not make an elision with the numbers 8 or 11.

Examples

[lə ɔ̃z mɛ]

[la ɥitjɛm ′nɥi]

[la ɔ̃zjɛm ʒœn fiːj]

le huit avril	April 8
le onze mai	May 11
le huitième jour	the eighth day
la huitième nuit	the eighth night
le onzième garçon	the eleventh boy
la onzième jeune fille	the eleventh girl

• Drop the vowel **i** of **si** *(if)* only in front of **il** *(he, it)* and **ils** *(they)*.

EXAMPLES

s'il te plaît	*please* (fam.)
s'il vous plaît	*please* (pl. and pol. s.)
Et s'il arrive?	*And what if he arrives?* **(arriver)**
	[But **Et si elle arrive?** And what if she arrives?]
Et s'ils insistent?	*And what if they insist?* **(insister)**
	[But **Et si elles insistent?** And what if they insist?]

Note that when **si** means *so,* there is never elision:

Elle est si innocente!	*She is so innocent!* **(être)**

• Do not make an elision if the word that follows begins with an aspirate **h.** Review the letter **h** in Lesson Seven.

EXAMPLES

le havre	*the harbor, the port*
la hauteur	*the height*
le héros	*the hero*
le haricot vert	*the green string bean*
la hutte	*the hut*

• Do not make an elision when there is a pause in speaking or if a phrase is set off by commas, a dash, or parentheses when written.

EXAMPLES

Elle n'est pas venue parce que, a-t-elle dit, elle n'avait pas le temps.	*She did not come because, said she, she didn't have the time.*

- Do not make an elision with the pronouns **le** or **la** when they are attached to the verb in the command (imperative form) and followed by a word beginning with a vowel.

EXAMPLES

Prononcez-le et écrivez-le aussi.	*Pronounce it and write it also.* **(prononcer, écrire)**
Prenez-la avec vous.	*Take it with you.* **(prendre)**

But there is an elision with **le** or **la** in front of **y:**

Mets-l'y.	*Put it there.* **(mettre)**

- Do not make an elision in the interrogative with inverted subject **je** and verb:

Ai-je assez d'argent?	*Do I have enough money?* **(avoir)**

But when not inverted, make an elision in **je:**

J'ai assez d'argent.	*I have enough money.* **(avoir)**

- Do not make an elision with **a** in **ça:**

Ça arrive de temps en temps.	*That happens from time to time.* **(arriver)**

- Do not make an elision with the vowel **i** in **qui:**

Qui est-ce qui a fait cela?	*Who is it who did that?* **(avoir, faire)**
Qu'est-ce qui est arrivé?	*What happened?* **(être)**

- There is often an elision with the vowel **u** in the personal pronoun **tu** when it is elided in familiar conversation. Instead of saying:

Tu as bien mangé?	*Did you eat well?*

You will often hear:

T'as bien mangé?

The e *muet*

$$[ə]$$

The **e muet** (silent e) occurs frequently in spoken French. When a group of syllables contains three **e muets,** pronounce one and do not pronounce the other two. If you do not pronounce any of the three, there will remain three successive consonants. In French, it would be awkward to pronounce three consonants without separating a syllable with the vowel **e.** In the following examples, the bar / through the vowel **e** means it is not pronounced.

[ʒtə ´di]

Jǝ te dis.   *I'm telling you.*

[It is preferable to suppress only the **e** in **je.** If you also suppressed the **e** in **te,** you would be left with three consonants in a row to pronounce: **j, t,** and **d.** That is avoided because the statement would not be articulated properly in good French pronunciation.]

[ʒtəl ´dɔn]

Jǝ te lǝ donne.   *I am giving it to you.*

[Here, **e** in **je** and **e** in **le** are suppressed. If you also suppressed the **e** in **te,** you would be left with four consonants in a row to pronounce: **j, t, l,** and **d.** That must be avoided.]

Jǝ voudrais   *I would like*
    unǝ livre dǝ beurrǝ,   *a pound of butter,*
    s'il vous plaît.   *please.*

[If you also suppressed **e** in **livre**, you would be left with four consonants in a row to pronounce: **v** and **r** in **livre**, **d** in **de**, and **b** in **beurre**. That would not be correct pronunciation.]

J'aimerais acheter un ballon rouge pour l'offrir à ce garçon.	*I'd like to buy a red balloon to offer it to this boy.*

Want to refresh your memory of the IPA phonetic symbols? How to read them? How to write them? How to pronounce them? Look again at pages ix–xii.

Listen carefully to the speakers pronounce a series of statements illustrating how to modulate your voice when asking a question, making a statement in the affirmative or negative, how to sound out exclamations, and how to speak in the imperative when telling someone to do or not to do something. During each pause, imitate the speaker's pronunciation, rhythm, intonation, accentuation, rise and fall of the voice, liaisons, elisions, nasal vowels, and suppressions of **e muet.** Don't hesitate to let yourself go and imitate the speaker!

Sample Questions

Bonjour! Comment allez-vous?	*Hello! How are you?*
Salut! Ça va?	*Hi! How are things?*
Veux-tu aller au cinéma avec moi?	*Do you want to go to the movies with me?*
Est-il neuf heures?	*Is it nine o'clock?*

Sample Answers in the Affirmative

Très bien, merci.	*Very well, thank you.*
Ça va, merci.	*Okay, thank you.*
Oui, j'aimerais bien aller au cinéma avec toi.	*Yes, I'd like very much to go to the movies with you.*
Oui, il est neuf heures.	*Yes, it's nine o'clock.*

Sample Answers in the Negative

Je ne me sens pas bien aujourd'hui.	*I don't feel well today.*
Non, je n'ai pas envie d'aller au cinéma.	*No, I don't feel like going to the movies.*
Non, il n'est pas neuf heures.	*No, it's not nine o'clock.*

Exclamatory Statements

C'est scandaleux!	*It's scandalous!*
C'est formidable!	*It's awesome!*
Chouette alors!	*That's cool!*
Et comment!	*And how!*
Quel mauvais temps!	*What bad weather!*
Comme elle est belle!	*How beautiful she is!*

Imperatives (Commands)

Taisez-vous!	*Be quiet!*
Apportez-moi un café crème, s'il vous plaît.	*Bring me a coffee with cream, please.*
Rends-le-moi, je te dis!	*Return it to me, I tell you!*
Ne faites pas cela!	*Don't do that!*
Occupez-vous de vos affaires!	*Mind your own business!*
N'y allez pas!	*Don't go there!*

PART FOUR
MORE PRACTICE
in CONTEXT FOR
ENRICHMENT

Part Four provides more practice in speaking French in context to improve your pronunciation: for example, popular phrases used frequently in conversational situations, proverbs, familiar sayings, paragraphs, dialogues, literary selections of French prose and poetry.

When you hear the following selections on the CD, repeat the French during the pauses. If the pauses are not long enough for you to remember all the words, you can always pause and start the CD at your convenience to hear a particular selection as often as you like.

The statements in French have been transcribed into the IPA phonetic symbols. Try pronouncing the symbols aloud as closely as you can to the French words printed right above them. Then check your pronunciation when you hear the French speakers on the CD. You will be pleased with your progress. It may be slow, but it will be steady and sure.

Use the English translation on the printed page to make sure you understand what you hear and what you are saying. The English words are not spoken on the CD.

Lesson Twelve
Popular French Phrases

Listen to the pronunciation of the French words on the CD and follow the sentences in French. Try to master the sound transcriptions under the French words. They are given in IPA phonetic symbols. Consult the guide to the phonetic symbols on pages ix–xii to review the symbols and sounds.

1. *Au contraire*, **mon ami, ce que tu dis n'est pas raisonnable.**

   [o kɔ̃ˈtrɛːr, mɔnaˈmi, skə ty di nɛ pɑ rɛzɔ̃ˈnabl]

   On the contrary, my friend, what you are saying is not reasonable.

2. **Comprenez-vous? Non,** *je regrette*, **je ne comprends pas.** *Répétez la question, s'il vous plaît.*

   [kɔ̃prəˈne vu, nɔ̃, ʒərˈgrɛt, ʒən kɔ̃prɑ̃ˈpɑ. repeˈte la kɛsˈtjɔ̃, sil vu plɛ]

   Do you understand? No, *I'm sorry*, I don't understand. *Repeat the question, please.*

3. *Combien ça coûte?*

   [kɔ̃ˈbjɛ̃ sa kut]

   How much does that cost?

4. *Quel en est le prix?*

   [kɛl ɑ̃ˈnɛ ləˈpri]

   What is the price of it?

5. *Si j'étais vous,* **je ne ferais pas ça.**

   [si ʒeteˈvu, ʒənˈfrɛ pɑ sa]

   If I were you, I wouldn't do that.

6. *Il faut réfléchir à deux fois avant d'agir.*

   [il fo refleˈʃir a dø fwa aˈvɑ̃ daˈʒiːr]

   Look before you leap. [You must think twice before acting.]

7. *D'ici la fin du mois, il fera beau temps.*

   [di´si la fɛ̃ dy mwɑ, il´fra bo tɑ̃]

   From now until the end of the month, the weather will be beautiful.

8. **Qu'est-ce que ça veut dire?**

   [kɛs´kə sa vø diːr]

   What does that mean?

9. **Quelles sont vos intentions, *au juste?***

   [kɛl sɔ̃ vozɛ̃tɑ̃´sjɔ̃, o ʒyst]

   What are your intentions, *exactly?*

10. **Bonsoir, Monsieur et Madame Durand.** *Comment allez-vous?*

    [bɔ̃´swaːr, mə´sjø e ma´dam dy´rɑ̃. kɔ´mɑ̃ tale´vu]

    Good evening, Mr. and Mrs. Durand. *How are you?*

11. ***Fort bien,* merci. Et vous?**

    [fɔːr bjɛ̃, mɛr´si. e vu]

    Quite well, thank you. And you?

12. ***Dès le début,* cette personne a dit des mensonges.**

    [dɛ lə de´by, sɛt pɛr´sɔn a´di de mɑ̃´sɔ̃ːʒ]

    From the very beginning, this person told lies.

---

chaise longue [ʃɛːz lɔ̃g] is often pronounced "shayz lounge" in English.

1. **Cueillez, cueillez votre jeunesse.** *Pierre de Ronsard*

   [kœ´je, kœ´je vɔtr ʒœ´nɛs]

   Gather, gather your youth.

   Gather ye roses while ye may. (Robert Louis Stevenson's *Gather Ye Roses*)

   Seize the day. (Horace's *Carpe diem*)

2. **Il pleut doucement sur la ville.** *Arthur Rimbaud*

   [il plø dusmã syr la vil]

   It is raining softly on the town.

3. **Il pleure dans mon coeur comme il pleut sur la ville.** *Paul Verlaine*

   [il plœːr dã mɔ̃ kœːr kɔm il plø syr la vil]

   It's raining tears in my heart as the rain falls on the town.

4. **Mais où sont les neiges d'antan?** *François Villon*

   [mɛ u sɔ̃ le nɛːʒ dã´tã]

   But where are the snows of yesteryear?

Il pleure dans mon coeur	**il plœːrə dã mɔ̃ kœːr**
Il pleure dans mon coeur	il plœːrə dã mɔ̃ kœːr
Comme il pleut sur la ville;	kɔm il plø syr la vil
Quelle est cette langueur	kɛl ɛ sɛtə lã´gœːr
Qui pénètre mon coeur?	ki pe´nɛtrə mɔ̃ kœːr
Ô bruit doux de la pluie	o brɥi du də la plɥi
Par terre et sur les toits!	par tɛːr e syr le twa
Pour un coeur qui s'ennuie	pur œ̃ kœːr ki sã´nɥi
Ô le chant de la pluie!	o lə ʃã də la plɥi

Il pleure sans raison	il plœːrə sɑ̃ reˊzɔ̃
Dans ce coeur qui s'écoeure.	dɑ̃ sə kœːr ki seˊkœːr
Quoi! Nulle trahison?…	kwa, nylə traiˊzɔ̃…
Ce deuil est sans raison.	sə dœːj ɛ sɑ̃ reˊzɔ̃
C'est bien la pire peine	sɛ bjɛ̃ la piːrə pɛn
De ne savoir pourquoi	də nə saˊvwaːr purˊkwa
Sans amour et sans haine	sɑ̃ zaˊmuːr e sɑ̃ ɛːn
Mon coeur a tant de peine!	mɔ̃ kœːr a tɑ̃ də pɛn

—Paul Verlaine   —pɔl verˊlɛn

Here's our literal translation to help you understand what you're pronouncing.

It's Raining Tears in My Heart

It's raining tears in my heart
As the rain falls on the town;
What is this languor
That cuts into my heart?

Oh, sweet sound of the rain
On the ground and on the rooftops!
For a heart that is weary
Oh, the song of the rain!

Tears are falling without reason
In this heart that is disheartened.
What? Not even a single betrayal?
This sorrow is without reason.

It is surely the worst sorrow
Not to know why
Without love and without hate
My heart feels so much sorrow.

—Paul Verlaine

LESSON FOURTEEN
PROVERBS, FAMILIAR SAYINGS, SELECTIONS FROM FRENCH LITERATURE, TONGUE TWISTERS, HUMOR, RIDDLES

Proverbs and familiar sayings

1. **Le chat parti, les souris dansent.**

   [lə ʃa par´ti, le su´ri dã:s]

   (The cat away, the mice dance.)

   When the cat is away, the mice will play.

2. **Qui se ressemble, s'assemble.**

   [ki srə´sãbl, sa´sãbl]

   (Those who are like each other gather together.)

   Birds of a feather flock together.

3. **Tout ce qui brille n'est pas or.**

   [tu ski brij nɛ pɑ ɔ:r]

   All that glitters is not gold.

4. **Sauve qui peut!**

   [sovki´pø]

   (Run away who can!)

   Run for your life!

5. **Les murs ont des oreilles.**

   [le my:r ɔ̃ dezɔ´rɛ:j]

   The walls have ears.

6. **Mieux vaut tard que jamais.**

   [mjø vo taːr kə ʒaˊmɛ]

   (Better it is worth late than never.)

   Better late than never.

7. **Plus ça change, plus c'est la même chose.**

   [ply sa ʃãːʒ, ply sɛ la mɛm ʃoːz]

   (The more that changes, the more it is the same thing.)

   The more things change, the more they remain the same.

8. **Aide-toi, le ciel t'aidera.**

   [ɛdˊtwa, lə sjɛl tɛdˊra]

   (Help yourself, heaven will help you.)

   Heaven helps those who help themselves.

9. **Il est bon de parler et meilleur de se taire.**

   [il ɛ bõ də parˊle e mɛˊjœːr də sə tɛːr]

   (It is good to speak and better to keep silent.)

   Speech is silver, silence is golden.

10. **Il n'y a pas de fumée sans feu.**

    [ilˊna pɑd fyˊme sã fø]

    (There isn't smoke without fire.)

    Where there's smoke, there's fire.

11. **Je chasse toujours les arcs-en-ciel.**

    [ʒə ʃas tuˊʒuːr leˊzark zã sjɛl]

    I'm always chasing rainbows.

    (Je me berce toujours d'illusions.)

    [ʒəmˊbɛrs tuˊʒuːr dilyˊzjõ]

    (I'm always deluding myself with illusions.)

12. **À tous ceux qu'il appartiendra**

    [a tu sø kil apartjɛ̃ˊdra]

    To Whom It May Concern

13. **À Dieu ne plaise!**

    [a djø nə plɛːz]

    God forbid!

14. **L'amour de l'argent est la racine de tous les maux.** *1 Timothy 6:10*

    [laˊmuːr də larˊʒɑ̃ ɛ la raˊsin də tu le mo]

    The love of money is the root of all evils.

15. **Et l'étymologie est la racine de tous les mots.** *T. Kendris*

    [e letimɔlɔˊʒi ɛ la raˊsin də tu le mo]

    And etymology is the root of all words.

16. **Être ou ne pas être. C'est toute la question.** Shakespeare (*Hamlet*)

    [ɛːtr u nə pɑˊzɛːtr. se tut la kɛstjɔ̃]

    To be or not to be. That is the question.

17. **Il faut cultiver notre jardin.** Voltaire (*Candide*)

    [il fo kyltiˊve nɔtrə ʒarˊdɛ̃]

    We must [it is necessary to] cultivate our garden.

18. **Revenons à nos moutons.**

    [rəvˊnɔ̃ a no muˊtɔ̃]

    Let's get back to our sheep.

    This is an expression that has come to mean "Let's get back to the subject, to what we were talking about." It's inspired by a line in *La Farce de Maistre Pathelin* (a medieval play): "Revenons à ces moutons" and by *Gargantua* (written by Rabelais during the Renaissance): "Retournant à noz moutons . . ."

19. **. . . car Dieu est amour.** *1 Jean 4:8*

    [kar djø etaˊmuːr]

    . . . for God is love.

20. **L'appétit vient en mangeant.**

    [lapeˊti vjɛ̃ ɑ̃ mɑ̃ˊʒɑ̃]

    Your appetite grows while you're eating.

How are you doing? Try reading the phonetic symbols on these pages aloud. They come out in French words!

21. **Honore ton père et ta mère, afin que tes jours se prolongent dans le pays que l'Éternel, ton Dieu, te donne.** *Exode 20:12 (des Dix Commandements)*

[ɔ´nɔːr tɔ̃ pɛːr e ta mɛːr, afɛ̃ kə te ʒuːr sə prɔ´lɔ̃ːʒ dɑ̃l pe´i kə leterˈnɛl, tɔ̃ djø, tə dɔn]

Honor your father and your mother, that your days may be long in the land which the Lord your God gives you.

22. **Tu ne tueras point.** *Exode 20:13 (des Dix Commandements)*

[ty nə tɥe´ra pwɛ̃]

You shall not kill.

23. **Heureux les miséricordieux, car ils obtiendront miséricorde.** *Matthieu 5:7*

[œ´rø le mizerikɔr´djø, kar il zɔptjɛ̃´drɔ̃ mizeri´kɔːrd]

Blessed are the merciful, for they shall obtain mercy.

24. **Il y a plus de bonheur à donner qu'à recevoir.** *Actes 20:35*

[ɪl´ja plyd bɔ´nœːr a dɔ´ne ka rəsə´vwaːr]

(There is more happiness in giving than receiving.)

It is more blessed to give than to receive.

25. **De leurs ennemis les sages apprennent bien des choses.** *Aristophane*

[də lœːr zɛn´mi le saːʒ a´prɛn bjɛ̃ de ʃoːz]

Wise persons learn many things from their enemies.

26. **Ils sont capables parce qu'ils se croient capables.** *Virgile*

[il sɔ̃ ka´pabl parskil sə krwa ka´pabl]

We are not all capable of everything.

27. **La raison est une lumière que Dieu a enflamée dans l'âme.** *Aristote*

[la re´zɔ̃ ɛtyn ly´mjɛːr kə djø a ɑ̃fla´me dɑ̃ lɑːm]

Reason is a light that God has kindled in the soul.

28. **Choisissez un travail que vous aimez et vous n'aurez pas à travailler un seul jour de votre vie.** *Confucius*

[ʃwazi´se œ̃ tra´vaːj kə vu zɛ´me e vu nɔ´re pɑ a trava´je œ̃ sœl ʒur də vɔtr vi]

Choose a job you love and you will never have to work a day in your life.

29. **Je ne suis pas Athénien ou Grec. Je suis un citoyen du monde.** *Socrate*

    [ʒən sɥi pɑ ateˊnjɛ̃ u grɛk. ʒə sɥi zœ̃ sitwaˊjɛ̃ dy mɔ̃ːd]

    I am not an Athenian or a Greek. I am a citizen of the world.

30. **Le coeur a ses raisons que la raison ne connaît point.** *Pascal (Les Pensées)*

    [lə kœːr a se reˊzɔ̃ kə la reˊzɔ̃ nə kuˊnɛ pwɛ̃]

    The heart has its reasons that reason does not know at all.

31. **Quand le vin entre, la raison sort.**

    [kɑ̃ lə vɛ̃ ɑ̃tr la reˊzɔ̃ sɔr]

    When wine goes in, reason (good sense) goes out.

32. **Quand le sage est en colère, il cesse d'être sage.**

    [kɑ̃ lə saʒ etɑ̃ kɔlɛr il sɛs dɛtr saʒ]

    When the wise man is angry, he stops being wise.

33. **Il faut battre le fer quand il est chaud.**

    [il fo batr lə fɛr kɑ̃ il ɛ ʃo]

    You have to strike while the iron is hot.

34. **Ne remets pas à demain ce que tu peux faire aujourd'hui.**

    [nə rəmɛ pɑ a dəmɛ̃ sə kə ty pø fɛr oʒurdɥi]

    Don't put off until tomorrow what you can do today.

35. **Il ne faut jamais vendre la peau de l'ours qu'on ne l'ait mis par terre.** *La Fontaine*

    [il nə fo ʒamɛ vɑ̃dr la po də lurs kɔ̃ nə lɛ mi par tɛr]

    (Never sell the bear's pelt until you've killed it.)

    Don't count your chickens before they're hatched.

---

déjà-vu [deʒa vy] (already seen) is often pronounced "déjà vous" (already you) in English.

Selections from French literature

1. The following well-known selection is from Act II, Scene IV of the classical comedy *Le Bourgeois Gentilhomme* by Molière. Repeat the French you hear during the pauses on the CD. The literal translation into English is given here so you will understand what you hear and what you repeat. The English words are not spoken on the CD.

In this scene, Monsieur Jourdain wants to learn about spelling so he can write a proper romantic note to the woman he loves and drop it at her feet. The Maître de Philosophie, the private tutor, is teaching Monsieur Jourdain the French vowels and how to pronounce them in preparation for the lesson in spelling.

Maître de Philosophie. Que voulez-vous donc que je vous apprenne?

(Master of Philosophy. So, what do you want me to teach you?)

M. Jourdain. Apprenez-moi l'orthographe.

(Mr. Jourdain. Teach me spelling.)

Maître de Philosophie. Très volontiers.

(Master of Philosophy. Very willingly.)

M. Jourdain. Après, vous m'apprendrez l'almanach, pour savoir quand il y a de la lune et quand il n'y en a point.

(Mr. Jourdain. Later, you will teach me the almanac so I can know when there is moonlight and when there isn't any.)

Maître de Philosophie. Soit. . . . Il faut commencer par une exacte connaissance de la nature des lettres et de la différente manière de les prononcer toutes. . . . J'ai à vous dire que les lettres sont divisées en voyelles, ainsi dites voyelles parce qu'elles expriment les voix; et en consonnes, ainsi appelées consonnes parce qu'elles sonnent avec les voyelles, et ne font que marquer les diverses articulations des voix. Il y a cinq voyelles ou voix: A, E, I, O, U.

(Master of Philosophy. So be it. . . . It is necessary to begin by an exact knowledge of the nature of the letters and of the different manner in pronouncing them all. . . . I have to tell you that the letters are divided into vowels; they are called vowels because they express the voices; and in consonants because they are sounded with the vowels and they simply mark the various articulations of the voices. There are five vowels or voices: A, E, I, O, U.)

M. Jourdain. J'entends tout cela.

Maître de Philosophie. La voix A se forme en ouvrant fort la bouche: A.

M. Jourdain. A. A. Oui.

Maître de Philosophie. La voix E se forme en rapprochant la mâchoire d'en bas de celle d'en haut: A, E.

M. Jourdain. A, E, A, E. Ma foi! Oui. Ah! que cela est beau!

Maître de Philosophie. Et la voix I en rapprochant encore davantage les mâchoires l'une de l'autre, et écartant les deux coins de la bouche vers les oreilles: A, E, I.

M. Jourdain. A, E, I, I, I, I. Cela est vrai. Vive la science!

Maître de Philosophie. La voix O se forme en rouvrant les mâchoires, et rapprochant les lèvres par les deux coins, le haut et le bas: O.

M. Jourdain. O, O. Il n'y a rien de plus juste. A, E, I, O, I, O. Cela est admirable! I, O, I, O.

Maître de Philosophie. L'ouverture de la bouche fait justement comme un petit rond qui représente un O.

M. Jourdain. O, O, O. Vous avez raison. O. Ah! La belle chose que de savoir quelque chose!

(Mr. Jourdain. I understand all that.)

(Master of Philosophy. The vowel A is formed by opening your mouth good and wide: A.)

(Mr. Jourdain. A. A. Yes.)

(Master of Philosophy. The vowel E is formed by bringing close together the lower jaw to the upper one: A, E.)

(Mr. Jourdain. A, E, A, E. My word! Yes. Ah! How beautiful that is!)

(Master of Philosophy. And the vowel I by bringing closer even more the lower jaw and the upper one, and by widening the two corners of the mouth [as in a broad smile] toward the ears [from ear to ear]: A, E, I.)

(Mr. Jourdain. A, E, I, I, I, I. That's true. Long live knowledge!)

(Master of Philosophy. The vowel O is formed by opening again the jaws, and by bringing closer to each other both corners of the lips, top and bottom [as in the shape of a circle]: O.)

(Mr. Jourdain. O, O. There is nothing more correct. A, E, I, O, I, O. That's admirable! I, O, I, O.)

(Master of Philosophy. The opening of the mouth is formed exactly like a little circle that represents an O.)

(Mr. Jourdain. O, O, O. You are right. O. Ah! How wonderful it is to know something!)

Maître de Philosophie. La voix U se forme en rapprochant les dents sans les joindre entièrement, et allongeant les deux lèvres en dehors, les approchant aussi l'une de l'autre sans les joindre tout à fait: U.

(Master of Philosophy. The vowel U is formed by bringing together the teeth without joining them entirely, and [at the same time] by thrusting both lips forward, and also bringing them both closer together without touching each other entirely: U.)

M. Jourdain. U, U. Il n'y a rien de plus véritable: U.

(Mr. Jourdain. U, U. There is nothing more truthful: U.)

Maître de Philosophie. Vos deux lèvres s'allongent comme si vous faisiez la moue; d'où vient que, si vous voulez la faire à quelqu'un, et vous moquer de lui, vous ne sauriez lui dire que: U.

(Master of Philosophy. Thrust your two lips forward as if you were pouting; if you want to pout at someone and make fun of the person, all you would have to say is: U.)

M. Jourdain. U, U. Cela est vrai. Ah! Que n'ai-je étudié plus tôt pour savoir tout cela?

(Mr. Jourdain. U, U. That is true. Ah! Why didn't I study sooner to know all that?)

Maître de Philosophie. Demain, nous verrons les autres lettres, qui sont les consonnes.

(Master of Philosophy. Tomorrow, we will see the other letters, which are the consonants.)

---

tout de suite [tud´sɥit] is often pronounced "toot sweet" in English.

2. The following selection is a paragraph of *Livre second* from *Émile ou de l'Éducation* by Jean-Jacques Rousseau. Repeat the French during the pauses.

Quand les enfants commencent à parler, ils pleurent moins. Ce progrès est naturel; un langage est substitué à l'autre. Sitôt qu'ils peuvent dire qu'ils souffrent avec des paroles, pourquoi le diraient-ils avec des cris, si ce n'est quand la douleur est trop vive pour que la parole puisse l'exprimer? S'ils continuent, alors, à pleurer, c'est la faute des gens qui sont autour d'eux. Dès qu'une fois Émile aura dit "J'ai mal," il faudra des douleurs bien vives pour le forcer de pleurer.

When children begin to speak, they cry less. This progress is natural; one language is substituted for another. As soon as they can say that they suffer in spoken words, why would they say so with cries, unless the pain is too sharp to be expressed in words? If they continue, then, to cry, it's the fault of the people who are around them. When once Émile has said, "I am hurting," only very sharp pains would force him to cry.

3. The following is from the beginning of a short story entitled *Un Coeur simple* in the collection *Trois Contes* by Gustave Flaubert. Repeat the French during the pauses.

Pendant un demi-siècle, les bourgeoises de Pont-l'Évêque envièrent à Madame Aubain sa servante Félicité.

Pour cent francs par an, elle faisait la cuisine et le ménage, cousait, lavait, repassait, savait brider un cheval, engraisser les volailles, battre le beurre, et resta fidèle à sa maîtresse qui, cependant, n'était pas une personne agréable.

For a half century, the bourgeois women of Pont-l'Évêque envied Madame Aubain her servant Felicity.

For one hundred francs a year, she did the cooking and the housework, she sewed, washed, ironed, knew how to bridle a horse, fatten the poultry, churn butter, and remained faithful to her mistress who, however, was not a pleasant person.

Tongue Twisters

Repeat these tongue twisters in French as fast as you can without getting your tongue twisted! The first one resembles the one in English that contains the repeated sounds of *sh* and *s*: for example, *She sells seashells by the seashore.*

1. **Le chasseur, sachant chasser sans son chien, chassera.**

   [lə ʃaˊsœːr, saˊʃɑ̃ ʃaˊse sɑ̃ sɔ̃ ʃjɛ̃, ʃasˊra]

   The hunter, knowing how to hunt without his dog, will hunt.

2. **Combien sont ces six saucissons-ci? Ces six saucissons-ci sont six sous. Si ces six saucissons-ci sont six sous, ces six saucissons-ci sont trop chers!**

   [kɔ̃ˊbjɛ̃ sɔ̃ se si sosiˊsɔ̃ si? se si sosiˊsɔ̃ si sɔ̃ si su. si se si sosiˊsɔ̃ si sɔ̃ si su, se si sosiˊsɔ̃ si sɔ̃ tro ʃer]

   How much are these six sausages? These six sausages cost six cents. If these six sausages cost six cents, these six sausages are too expensive!

3. **Tas de riz, tas de rats. Tas de riz tentant, tas de rats tentés.**

   [tɑ də ri, tɑ də ra. tɑ də ri tɑ̃tɑ̃, tɑ də ra tɑ̃te]

   Pile of rice, pile of rats. Tempting pile of rice, pile of tempted rats.

4. **Si ton tonton tond ton tonton, ton tonton sera tondu.**

   [si tɔ̃ tɔ̃tɔ̃ tɔ̃ tɔ̃ tɔ̃tɔ̃, tɔ̃ tɔ̃tɔ̃ sra tɔ̃ˊdy]

   If your uncle cuts your uncle's hair, your uncle will have short hair.

Humor (*Jeux de Mots*/Word Games)

1. Pronounce the word **MAISON.** Now scramble the letters and find another French word. Print it here on the short lines __ __ __ __ __ __. Now pronounce the new French word. The answer is on the next page.

2. Play the same game for this word: **VARIER**

   __ __ __ __ __ __

3. Pronounce the French word **ou**, which means *or*. Write the appropriate accent mark on the required letter of that word and get another word. Write the new word and the meaning of the new word in English on this line _____. Now pronounce the new French word.

4. Pronounce the French word **la foi**, which means *faith*. Add one letter in that word and get a new word. Write the new word and its meaning in English on this line _____. Now pronounce the new French word.

5. Pronounce the French word **la rue**, which means *street*. Now add one letter in that word and get a new word. Write the new word and its meaning in English on this line _____. Now pronounce the new French word.

NOTE: Here are the answers to the word games in the previous exercise.

1. AIMONS/*Let's love* **2. ARRIVE**/as in **J'arrive!** (*I'm coming!*) or **Il/Elle/On arrive!** (*He/She/It is coming!*)
3. où/*where* **4. la fois**/*time, as in one time, last time*
5. la roue/*wheel*

Riddles—(*Les Devinettes*) [le dəvi´nɛt]

1.

Quelle est la chose la plus sale de la maison?

[kɛl ɛ la ʃoːz la ply sal də la mɛ´zɔ̃]

What is the dirtiest thing in the house?

un balai / a broom
[œ̃ ba´lɛ]

2.

> **J'ai un chapeau, mais je n'ai pas de tête. Ne trouvez-vous pas que c'est bête? Que suis-je?**
>
> [ʒe œ̃ ʃa´po mɛ ʒə ne pa də tɛt. nə tru´ve vu pa kə sɛ bɛt. kə sɥiːʒ]
>
> I have a hat, but I don't have a head. Don't you think that's stupid? What am I?
>
> *un champignon* / a mushroom
> [œ̃ ʃɑ̃pi´ɲɔ̃]

3.

> **J'ai des yeux mais je n'ai pas de paupières et je vis dans l'eau. Qui suis-je?**
>
> [ʒe de zyø mɛ ʒə ne pad po´pjɛːr e ʒə vi dɑ̃ lo. ki sɥiːʒ]
>
> I have eyes but I don't have eyelids and I live in water. Who am I?
>
> *un poisson* / a fish
> [œ̃ pwa´sɔ̃]

Helpful Mnemonic Tips:
Ways to Remember Sounds,
Pronunciations, Spellings

Mnemonic Tips

1. To remember that there are only four nasal vowels in French, hang on to this catchy phrase because each word contains one of the four nasal vowels:

   un bon vin blanc / a good white wine

   [œ̃ bɔ̃ vɛ̃ blɑ̃]

2. If you keep pronouncing **un oeuf** / an egg incorrectly, and you want to get it right, say this aloud:
   Do you want one egg? Two eggs?
   One egg is enough!
   One egg is **un oeuf!**

   [œ̃ nœf]

3. If you don't know which is the *accent aigu* (acute) (*é*) and which is the *accent grave* (*è*), remember that the patient died of acute appendicitis (*é*) and ended up in the grave (*è*).

4. If you have difficulty with the spellings, meanings, and pronunciation of **vieille, veille, vieil,** and **vieux,** remember the following catchy phrase:

   > **La vieille dame a passé la veille de Noël avec son vieil ami dans un vieux cabaret en joyeuse compagnie d'un jeune valet.**
   >
   > [la vjɛːj dam a pɑ́se la vɛːj de nɔ́ɛl avɛk sɔ̃ vj´ɛj a´mi dɑ̃ zœ̃ kaba´rɛ ɑ̃ ʒwa´jøːz kɔ̃pa´ɲi dœ̃ ʒœn va´lɛ]
   >
   > The old lady spent Christmas Eve with her old male friend in an old cabaret in the cheerful company of a young valet.

5. The verb **mourir** [muˊriːr] (to die) has one **r** because a person dies once; but **nourrir** [nuˊriːr] (to nourish) has two **r**'s because a person is nourished more than once.

6. The verb **perdre** [pɛrdr] (to lose) is related to the English word *perdition*; in theology, perdition is a place for lost souls. The pronunciation of the English *to lose* sounds very much like the pronunciation of Toulouse, a city in the southwest of France. Have you listened to the CD today? There's no time Toulouse!

7. Pronounce **bonne** [bɔn] (*maid* or *good*, f.s.) as in the English word *bun*. Just remember that the maid brought us a tray of good buns.

8. In French, if you don't know your right, **droite** [drwat], from your left, **gauche** [goːʃ], notice that **droite** contains "it" and so does "right." Also, if you're maladroit you're clumsy (unless you're left-handed!).

9. You go away when you **partir** [parˊtiːr] and you go out when you **sortir** [sɔrˊtiːr]. If you're not sure of the precise meaning of those two words, remember that **partir** and **away** contain the vowel **a**. Note, too, that **sortir** and **go out** contain the vowel **o**.

10. If you are not sure of **le gâteau** [lə gɑˊto] (cake) and **le bateau** [lə baˊto] (boat) because you can't remember which one requires the circumflex accent, remember that the accent mark ˆ in **gâteau** is the icing on top of the cake!

BASIC RULES of Division of Syllables in FRENCH

A syllable in a word is a unit of pronunciation that consists of a single sound. You can learn to divide words correctly into syllables to achieve better pronunciation and better skill in spelling words.

Basic Rules with Examples

1. A syllable must contain a vowel. It may contain only one vowel and one or more consonants or no consonant.

French Word	IPA Phonetic Symbols	Division into Syllables	English Meaning
école	[e ´kɔl]	é / cole	*school*

2. When you are dealing with single separate consonants, each consonant remains with the vowel that follows it.

beaucoup	[bo ´ku]	beau / coup	*many, much*

3. When two consonants come together, they are separated; the first remains with the preceding syllable and the second remains with the following syllable.

important	[ɛ̃ pɔr ´tɑ̃]	im / por / tant	*important*

But if the second of the two consonants that come together is *l* or *r,* do not separate them:

immeuble	[im ´mœ bl]	im / meu / ble	*apartment building*
après	[a ´prɛ]	a / près	*after*

4. When three consonants come together, the first two remain with the preceding vowel and the third remains with the vowel that follows it.

institut   [ɛ̃ ti ´ty]   ins / ti / tut   *institute*

But if the third of the three consonants that come together is *l* or *r,* do not separate that third consonant from the second; it remains with the second consonant.

comprendre [kɔ̃ ´prɑ̃ dr] com / pren / dre *to understand*

Vowel Sounds

Two vowels together are generally separated if they are strong vowels (**a, e, o**).

aéroport   [a e ro ´pɔr] a / é / ro / port *airport*

But if you are dealing with a weak vowel (**i, u**), it ordinarily remains in the same syllable with its neighboring vowel, especially if that other vowel is a strong vowel.

huître   [ɥi tr]   hui / tre   *oyster*

If you have not been practicing everything in this book and on the CDs, just start all over again from the beginning because that old cliché, "Practice makes perfect!" is true. And you will surely see a pronounced improvement.

Appendix

Index of Key French Words Used in This Book and on the CDs

This index will help you find common French words as well as popular phrases and idiomatic expressions from all the lessons in this book. The most important ones are printed in **boldface.**

Verbs in the infinitive form and in a variety of frequently used tenses are also included. Many of them are used in phrases, expressions, and complete statements, some of which, we hope, are humorous. Others are used in excerpts of selections from French literature, in proverbs, familiar quotations, sayings, riddles, and tongue twisters. They are also printed in **boldface** so you can spot them easily.

If any of the French words, phrases, idiomatic expressions, familiar quotations, or verb form entries in this index arouse your curiosity and interest, turn to the page reference and see how they are used, how they are expressed in written phonetic symbols for proper pronunciation, how they are translated into English, and how they sound on the CDs. To review unfamiliar or difficult French verbs in the infinitive form or in verb tense forms that you see in this index, consult the popular book *501 French Verbs*, published by Barron's. It contains verbs that are fully conjugated in all the tenses as well as many other features to help you in your French studies.

Words, Phrases, and Idiomatic Expressions

Q

Index of French Written Forms Presented in This Book

This index will help you find French words that contain certain orthographical groups of letters that are challenging to pronounce properly. Of course this index does not contain all the different written forms of words in the French language. If it did, it would be voluminous. If you do not find the part of a word whose spelling is difficult to pronounce, look up the French word in the Index of Key French Words (p. 171). If the French word you are looking for is not in either of the two indexes, write us a letter care of Barron's Educational Series, Inc. We would be glad to consider including the French words you suggest in a future edition.

This book with CDs is a basic source that contains over two thousand important everyday words requiring a vast variety of pronunciations. In this index you will find an alphabetical listing of a variety of different forms written as single letters or as clusters of letters and syllables. We have made an analytical study of the different parts of a French word to help you master the art of French pronunciation. Such varieties of written forms are found in different positions in French words: for example, in words of one syllable and in words of more than one syllable in the beginning (initial), middle, or ending (final) position of a French word. After you have mastered the basic principles of French pronunciation, you will enjoy pronouncing French words, phrases, expressions, and sentences properly.

Column 1 shows the different written forms arranged alphabetically. Column 2 tells you the position of the written form in a particular French word. Column 3 lists examples of words that contain the written forms, and Column 4 gives you the page reference to find the examples as well as additional words containing the same written forms. It is on those pages where you will also find the IPA phonetic symbols. You can also hear the pronunciation on the CDs and repeat them during the pauses.

For example, if you want to know how to pronounce a word that contains the syllable *aille*, as in the word *taille*, or a word that contains the syllable *euil*, as in the word *écureuil*, look it up in the alphabetical list of written forms here and note the examples and corresponding page references.

To help improve your pronunciation of French, this index also contains many written forms found in French verb tenses used in sentences. They appear in this index as infinitives: for example, **avoir, être, aimer, rompre**. To review all the verb forms listed here for pronunciation purposes, consult Barron's *501 French Verbs*. It contains fully conjugated verbs in all the tenses as well as many other helpful features.

Written Forms	Position in Word	Examples	Page Number
a	in one syllable	la, ma, sa, ta	4
	in middle position	patte, Paris	ix
	in final position	collage, papa	ix
à	in initial, middle, or final position	à, là, çà, déjà-vu, voilà, là-bas, holà	13 13
â	in initial or middle position	âge, grâce, château, câble, blâme pâtisserie hâte, pâte, pâtes	ix, 4, 92 13, 92 50 ix, 14, 92
abs	**b** + **s** is sounded *ps*	absent, absente, absolument	100
ac	in final position when the letter **c** is not pronounced. But there are exceptions, as in **le bac, le bec**. See the consonant **c**.	estomac, tabac	102
acc	in initial position, **acc + a, o, u** is sounded *ak*	accabler, accuser, accord, accourir	103 103
	in initial position, **acc + e, i** is sounded *aks*	accident, accepter accès	103
aël	in final syllable	Israël	16
aën	in one syllable	Camille Saint-Saëns	26, 93
ai	in one-syllable word	gai, j'ai (**avoir**) mai, aime (**aimer**) vrai	ix, xi, 22 6 23
	in second of two syllables	balai	23
	in final syllable (verb forms)	j'irai (**aller**) je parlerai (**parler**)	22 22
aî	in one-syllable word	la chaîne	24
	in middle position	l'enchaînement	vi, 139
aï	in accentuated syllable	naïf	19
aid	in one-syllable word	laid	23

Written Forms	Position in Word	Examples	Page Number
aie	in one-syllable word (verb form)	je paie (**payer**)	77
aient	in final syllable (verb forms)	ils allaient (**aller**) elles iraient (**aller**)	23 23
aies	in one-syllable word (verb form)	tu paies (**payer**)	77
ail	in final syllable	travail	23
aile	in one-syllable word	l'aile	23, 111
aille	in one-syllable word or final position	la taille il/elle travaille (verb form **travailler**)	4 23
aillent	in final position	ils/elles travaillent (verb form of **travailler**)	23
aim	in one-syllable word	faim	90, 92
aime	in one-syllable word	j'aime (verb form of **aimer**)	ix
ain	in one-syllable word in final syllable	main romain	91, 92 91
aine	in final position	capitaine, douzaine Jean de La Fontaine africaine, certaine	24 24 24
aîne	in one-syllable word	la chaîne	24
aint	in one syllable or final position	saint	91
aire	in final position	anniversaire dictionnaire ordinaire extraordinaire	24 24 24 24
ais	in one-syllable word or in final position	mais je vais (verb form of **aller**) français, je parlais je parlerais (verb forms of **parler**) je fais (**faire**) je sais (**savoir**)	ix, 6, 24 90, 92 25, 90, 92 24, 25 25 25 90, 92 90, 92
aïs	in accentuated syllable	maïs	19
aise	in final position	mayonnaise	83
ait	in one-syllable word or final	lait il parlait, elle parlerait (verb forms of **parler**)	25 25

Written Forms	Position in Word	Examples	Page Number
aît	in final position	il paraît (**paraître**) s'il vous plaît (**plaire**)	25 25
aix	in one-syllable word in initial position	paix Aix-en Provence Aix-la-Chapelle Aix-les-Bains	25 25 25 25
al	in final position	cheval	103
am	in initial position	ambassade, ambiance, ambulance	93 93
amme	in one syllable in final position	gramme programme télégramme	25 25 25
an	in one-syllable word in final position	blanc, dans, sans, ange, chant roman	93, 94 93 93
anc	in one-syllable word or in final position	blanc, banc, franc	x, 102
ant	in one-syllable word or in final position	chant, gant, géant extravagant	93, 108 123
aoû	in one-syllable word	août	ix, 26
ap	in one-syllable word	rap	113
ard	in one-syllable word or in final position	tard	154
ars	in one-syllable word or in final position	mars	26
as	in middle of word in one syllable in final position	bas-relief tu as, le pas, l'as je ne sais (**savoir**) pas embarras, Edgar Degas	4 26 26 26
asse	in middle of word	passeport	4
at	in final position	chat, chocolat	103
ation	in final position	prononciation, articulation	121 158
au	in one syllable in initial position	au café au lait gauche automne	27, 30 27 ix, 8 62
aud	in one-syllable word in accentuated final syllable	chaud costaud, Rimbaud	27 27
aul	in one-syllable word or final	Paul	ix, 9

Written Forms	Position in Word	Examples	Page Number
aule	in one-syllable word or final	Paule	8
aut	in one-syllable word final position	haut, il faut (**falloir**) artichaut, Truffaut	27 27
aux	in one-syllable word or final position	aux chevaux, journaux	27 ix, 8, 27
aye	in one-syllable word (verb form)	je paye (**payer**)	76
ayer	in final position (infinitives)	**balayer, bégayer, essayer, payer**	77 77
ayes	in one-syllable word (verb form)	tu payes (**payer**)	76
ayez	in final position (verb forms)	vous ayez (**avoir**) balayez (**balayer**) bégayez (**bégayer**) essayez (**essayer**) payez (**payer**)	77 77 77 77 77
ays	in one-syllable word in initial position	pays paysage	78 78
b	in initial, middle, or final syllable position	beau, ambulance, alphabet	88, 93 44
bs	**b** + **s** is sounded *ps*	absent, absolument	100
c	final **c** is **k** sound	avec, bec, bac, mec, pic, parc, choc, public Toulouse-Lautrec Cadillac porc-épic Québec	101 101, 102 101 101 102 114
	final **c** is silent, mute (**muet**) **c** preceded by **e** and followed by **o** (**eco**) is sounded as hard *g*	porc, banc, blanc estomac, tabac second, seconde, secondaire	102 102 102 102
ç + a, o, u	in any position (*s* sound)	ça, français prononçons, reçu	24, 101, 149 101
ca	initial (*k* sound)	café, caractère	xi, 100
cc + e, i	initial (first syllable) (*aks* sound)	accident, accès, accepter	103 103
cc + a, o, u	initial (first syllable) (*ak* sound)	accabler, accuser, accord, accourir	103 103
ce	in initial syllable (*s* sound)	cela	100, 101

Written Forms	Position in Word	Examples	Page Number
ch	in initial syllable (*k* sound)	chaos, choeur, chorégraphie	104 104
	in middle syllable (*k* sound)	orchestre, écho	104
	in initial syllable (*sh* sound)	chat, cheval, chimie, chocolat, chute, chou chaise, chose	103 103 xii
	in middle position (*sh* sound)	Vichy, parachute l'enchaînement	103 vi, 139
ci	in initial (*s* sound)	cinéma	100, 185
	in middle (*s* sound)	ici	ix, 7, 136
co	in initial position	colis, courage	100
coe	in one-syllable word	coeur	59, 115, 151, 152
ct	final **ct** is *kt* sound	correct, direct	29
	final **ct** is silent, mute (**muet**)	aspect, respect	30
cu	in initial position	curiosité	100
d	in initial position	depuis, dent	84, 93
	in final position silent, mute (**muet**)	bord, nord, nid, froid, poids	104 50, 60, 61
	in final position **d** is sounded	sud	104
	d is sounded as *t*	grand amour, grand homme, quand elle parle	105 105 105
e	in one-syllable word mute e (**e muet**)	je, de, le, me, se, te	x, 5
e	initial in one-syllable word	elle	6
é	any position: initial, middle, or final	café, thé, dé bébé, été, allé, âgé chrétienne	ix, 6 xi, 14 35
è	in initial position	ère	38
	in middle position	poème, poète	ix, 6
	in final position	dernière	38
	one syllable	mère, père, frère	15
ê	in any position	tête, forêt, vêpres prêt, bête, fête	ix, 6, 16 16
ë	in final position	Noël, Israël, Citroën	16
eau	in any accentuated position	eau, Jean Cocteau, bateau, chapeau, gâteau, marteau	ix, 8, 29 29, 89 29
	in one-syllable word	beau	88, 89, 150

Written Forms	Position in Word	Examples	Page Number
eaux	in any accentuated position	eaux, bateaux, chapeaux, gâteaux, marteaux	8, 29, 89 29 29
ect	in final position **ct** is sounded **ct** is not sounded	correct, direct, infect infect, intellect aspect, respect	29, 30 30 30
ée	in one-syllable word accentuated final	fée dictée, idée, lycée elle est allée (**aller**)	30 30 30
ées	in one-syllable word accentuated final	fées dictées, idées, lycées elles sont allées (**aller**)	30 30 30
ei	in one-syllable word	neige, seize, peine	31
eil	in accentuated final position	orteil, réveil, soleil pareil, vermeil	31 31
eils	in accentuated final position	orteils, réveils, soleils	31
eille	in accentuated final position in one-syllable word	pareille, abeille, corbeille, oreille Marseille, Corneille veille, veille de Noël	31 31 32 83
eilles	in accentuated final position	abeilles	31
ein	in one-syllable word	sein	91, 92
ël	in final position	Noël, Israël	16
elle	in final position in one-syllable word	chapelle, cruelle, quelle, appelle (**appeler**), réelle elle, belle	32 32 ix, 32
em	in initial position in middle position	empire, emploi exemple	93 93
emme	in one-syllable word in accentuated final position	flemme, gemme femme dilemme	34 xi, 35 34
ën	in final position	Citroën	16
en	in final position in one-syllable word in initial position	citoyen, examen dent, cent, pente ennemi	92 93 93
enne	in accentuated final position in initial position	antenne, lycéenne, européenne ennemi	35 35 93

Written Forms	Position in Word	Examples	Page Number
ent	in final position	**elles parlent, elles écrivent,**	35
	of a verb form	**elles travaillent, ils écoutent**	36
		ils content	94
	in one-syllable word in final position	cent, dent argent, excellent	93 123, 131
	in final position in an adjective, (m.s.)	il est content, absent	94 100
er	in final position of an infinitive	jouer, parler, donner, chercher	ix, 6, 36 36
	in final position of two-syllable word	enfer, scooter, super, rocher	37 6
	in middle position	merci, éternel, ferme service, cherche	ix, 37, 38 38
ère	in one-syllable word	ère, chère, mère, père, frère	38 38
erie	in final syllable	papeterie, pâtisserie	50
erre	in one-syllable word	il erre (**errer**), terre, guerre	39 39
es	in one-syllable word in verb form	mes, tes, ses, les, des tu es (**être**)	6, 39 39
ès	in one-syllable word	très, dès, ès (Licence **ès** Lettres)	40
	in final position	progrès, excès, accès, Mendès-France, Pierre, Sainte Agnès	40 40 40
ess	in initial position	essai, essence, essayer essuie-glace, essuie-main	41 41
est	in one-syllable noun in one-syllable verb form	est (east), ouest (west) est, est-ce, c'est, est-ce que, qu'est-ce que	41 41 41
et	in final position	jouet, valet, cabaret alphabet, ballet, carnet, bonnet, paquet, ticket poulet, sommet, gourmet	ix, 6, 165 xi, 44 44 44
	in one syllable	net, Le Net	121
	in one-syllable (conjunction)	et	44
ette	in final position	devinette, étiquette, omelette	45 45

Written Forms	Position in Word	Examples	Page Number
eu	(verb forms of **avoir**)	eu, il eut	10, 45
		j'ai eu	x, 45
	in one-syllable word	peu, feu, jeu, bleu	x, 45
	in middle position	peuple	x
	in final position	aveu, neveu	45
eub	in one-syllable word	meubles	47
eue	in one-syllable word	queue	x
euf	in one-syllable word	neuf, veuf	x, 47
euil	in final position	écureuil, fauteuil	47
	in one-syllable word	deuil, seuil	47, 48
euille	in one-syllable word	feuille, feuilles	48
	in final position	portefeuille	48
eul	in one-syllable word	seul, seuls	47
eule	in one-syllable word	seule, seules, gueule	47
eune	in one-syllable word	jeune	x
eur	in one-syllable word	peur, fleur, leur, heure	x, 46, 47, 87, 88
	in final position	bonheur, ordinateur	46, 88
eus	in one-syllable word	bleus	46
euse	in one-syllable word	creuse	46
	in final position	crémeuse, hideuse,	46
		nerveuse	46
eut	in one-syllable word	il peut (**pouvoir**),	46
	(verb forms)	il pleut (**pleuvoir**)	46
		il eut (**avoir**)	x, 45
euve	in one-syllable word	veuve, fleuve,	47
	in verb forms	qu'il pleuve (**pleuvoir**)	47
		ils peuvent (**pouvoir**)	47
	in final position	épreuve	47
		Catherine Deneuve	47
eux	in one-syllable word	ceux, yeux, feux,	x, 46
		jeux, deux	11, 46
	in verb form	je peux (**pouvoir**)	46
	in final position	cheveux	46
ey	in final position	jockey, disc-jockey,	78
		volley	78
ez	in one-syllable word	nez, chez	48, 125
	in final syllable	assez	125
	in verb form ending	vous avez (**avoir**)	48
		vous allez (**aller**)	48
		vous parlez (**parler**)	48, 125
		vous prononcez (**prononcer**)	48, 125

Written Forms	Position in Word	Examples	Page Number
f	in initial position; pronounce *f*	foi	107
	in final position; pronounce *f*	chef, neuf, veuf soif, oeuf, boeuf, informatif	107 x, 58, 107 107
	in middle position; pronounce *f*	informatif	107
	in final position, **f** is silent, mute **(muet)**	clef, chef-d'oeuvre, oeufs, boeufs	107 58, 107
	f is pronounced *v*	neuf ans, il est neuf heures	108
g	**g + a, o, u** is hard *g*	garage, gant, gomme, guère, guerre, gueule	xi, 108 108
	g + e, i, y is soft *g*	géant, Georges, gilet, gymnastique, garage	108 xii, 108
gn	in middle position	agneau, signer oignon, signal	xi 109
	in final syllable	montagne, Alfred de Vigny	109
	But in middle position hard **g + n** in two separate sounds	diagnostique	109
h	when silent, mute **(muet)**	hôpital, hospitalité, hôte hôtesse, hôtel	109 109
	when aspirate **(aspiré)**	hors, hors-d'oeuvre, dehors h aspiré	109 109, 110, 137, 139
		Le Havre, le haut, le haricot	110
i	in accentuated position	ici, ami, il, ski	ix, 7
î	in accentuated position	île fit, huître	ix, 7, 18 18
ï	in accentuated position	héroïsme, maïs, Moïse, égoïste, naïf	19 19
id	in one-syllable word	nid	50
ie	in accentuated final syllable	dynastie, géographie papeterie, pâtisserie	50 50
	in one-syllable word	vie	50
ied	in one-syllable word	pied	51, 83
ieds	in one-syllable word	pieds	51

Written Forms	Position in Word	Examples	Page Number
ieille	in one-syllable word	vieille	83
ième	in final position of a two-syllable word	deuxième, douzième	52
ien	in one-syllable word	bien, rien	92
ienne	in one-syllable word	chienne	35
	in accentuated final position	chrétienne, Parisienne	35
ier	in final position	dernier, premier, acier	x, 11, 36
		pompier	36
		papier, cahier	51
	in one-syllable word	fier, hier	11, 37
ière	in one-syllable word	fière	38
	in final position of a two-syllable word	première, dernière, prière	38, 52; 38, 52
ières	in final position of a two-syllable word	prières, premières	52
iers	in final position	derniers, premiers	52
		cahiers, papiers	52
ies	in accentuated final syllable	boulangeries	50
ieu	in one-syllable word	lieu	x, 11, 83
il	in one-syllable word	il, cil, fil	ix, 53
	in final position of two-syllable word	fusil, outil, gentil	53, 54
ille	in one-syllable word	fille, ville	54, 83
	in final position of two-syllable word	cédille, famille, gentille	54
illes	in one-syllable word	filles, villes	54
	in final position of two-syllable word	cédilles, familles, gentilles	54; 54
ils	in one-syllable word	ils, cils, fils	53
	in final position of two-syllable word	fusils, outils, gentils,	53, 54
im	in first syllable of word	simple	91, 92
imm	in initial position	immeuble	167
in	in one-syllable word	vin, fin	x, 90, 92, 94
ing	in final position	camping	xi
inq	in one-syllable word	cinq	xi
ique	in final position in a word of two or more syllables	boutique, élastique, pacifique, publique	55; 55, 102

Written Forms	Position in Word	Examples	Page Number
iques	in final position in a word of two or more syllables	boutiques, élastiques, pacifiques	55 55
ire	in one-syllable word	lire, dire	ix
is	in one-syllable word	gris	50
	in verb forms	dis (**dire**), lis (**lire**), suis (**être**)	50 51
	in final position of two-syllable word	Paris, avis, souris,	ix, 50, 51
ît	in an accentuated position	fît (verb form of **faire**) huître, île	18 7, 18
it	in one-syllable word	le lit	51
	in verb forms	écrit (**écrire**), lit (**lire**) dit (**dire**)	51 51
ix	in final position of two-syllable word	perdrix	51
	in one-syllable word	prix, six, dix	51
iz	in one-syllable word	riz	51
j	in one-syllable word	je, Jean, Jeanne, jouer, je joue	xii, 110 110
l	in initial position	Lily, le lis, le lys, il lit (**lire**), le lit	111 111
	in final position	bal, sel, final	xi, 111
ll	in one-syllable word	elle, belle, ville, mille salle, selle	111 111
	in middle position	ballet, bulletin	xi, 111
m	in initial position	ma, me, madame	x, xi, 5
	in middle position	aimable, jamais	134, 154
mm	in middle position	comment	146
	in one-syllable word	comme, homme, pomme	62
n	in initial position	neuf	x, 47
	in middle position	cinéma, banane	xi, 145, 146
nn	in initial and middle positions	anniversaire, dictionnaire	24
o	in any accentuated position	rose, pot, vidéo	8
ô	in any accentuated position	pôle, allô cône, dôme	ix, 8 19
	in initial position	hôte, hôtel	19, 109
obe	in one-syllable or final position	robe	9
ode	in one-syllable word	mode	ix

Written Forms	Position in Word	Examples	Page Number
oeil	in one-syllable in initial position	oeil oeillade, oeillet	57, 83 57
oël	in final position	Noël	16
oën	in final position	Citroën	16
oeu	in one-syllable word	voeu	58
oeud	in one-syllable word	noeud	x, 58
oeuds	in one-syllable word	noeuds	58
oeuf	in one-syllable word	oeuf, boeuf	x, 58
oeufs	in one-syllable word	oeufs, boeufs	58
oeur	in one-syllable word	coeur, Sacré-Coeur, soeur, belle-soeur	59, 115 59, 151
oeuvre	in one-syllable word	oeuvre, oeuvre d'art, hors-d'oeuvre, chef-d'oeuvre	59 59 59
oeux	in one-syllable word	voeux, meilleurs voeux	58
oi	in one-syllable word initial position in a two-syllable word	moi, toi, soi, soir, loi, foi, roi, soif, noir, poire poireau, poireux, Hercule Poirot, emploi	60 60 60 60 93
oid	in one-syllable word	froid	60
oids	in one-syllable word	poids	61
oie	in one-syllable word	oie, foie, soie	61
oigt	in one-syllable word	doigt	61
ois	in one-syllable word in verb forms	fois, mois, pois je dois (**devoir**) je crois (**croire**) je bois (**boire**) je vois (**voir**)	61 61 61 61 61
oïs	in accentuated syllable	héroïsme, égoïste, Moïse	19 19
oit	in one-syllable word in verb forms	toit il doit (**devoir**) elle croit (**croire**) soit	61 61 61 61
oix	in one-syllable word	croix, noix	61
om	in one-syllable word	nom, bombe	89
omme	in one-syllable word	comme, somme, homme pomme	62 62, 89
ommes	in one-syllable word in verb form	hommes, pommes nous sommes (**être**)	62, 89 62
omne	in final syllable	automne	62

Written Forms	Position in Word	Examples	Page Number
omps ompt	*p* in **omps**, **ompt** is silent, mute (**muet**)	je romps (**rompre**) je compte (**compter**)	113 113
on	in one-syllable word	bon, on, mon, non bonbons	x 89, 90, 94, 132, 134
one	in final syllable	téléphone, anglophone, monotone, francophone	62 62, 90
	in verb form	je téléphone (**téléphoner**)	62
onne	in one-syllable word or final syllable	donne, tonne, bonne, couronne, personne	ix, xi, 90 63, 90
	in verb forms	je donne (**donner**) le téléphone sonne (**sonner**)	9, 63 63 63
op	in one-syllable word or final position	trop, galop, sirop, hop! bop, be-bop pop, stop	63, 112 113 113
or	in one-syllable word or final position	or, alors, port, porte	ix, 9
ort	in one-syllable word	mort	ix
os	in one-syllable word or final position	dos, gros, nos, vos, os propos, chaos, héros, albatros repos	64 64 64 ix, 8, 64
osse	in one-syllable word or final position	bosse, gosse, grosse Écosse	65 65
ot	in one-syllable word	mot, pot dot	ix, 8, 65 66, 121
	in final position	abricot, canot, tricot, Alfred Cortot	65 65
ôt	in one-syllable word in final position	tôt aussitôt, bientôt, plutôt	8, 66 66
otte	in one-syllable word in final position	botte, flotte jupe-culotte, carotte	66 66
ou	in one-syllable word in initial position in final position	ou, cou, fou, chou, coude toucher, pousser, tousser genou, yaourt	ix, xi, 69 69 69
où	in one-syllable word	où	20, 69
oua	in initial position	ouate, ouaté, ouater	61
oue	in one-syllable word in verb form	roue, boue, joue je joue (**jouer**), **louer** jouet, ouest	ix, 69 69, 84 x, 84
oui	in one-syllable word	oui, Louis, Louise	x, 84

Written Forms	Position in Word	Examples	Page Number
ouille	in one-syllable word	nouille	71
	in final syllable	grenouille, citrouille	71
ouilles	in one-syllable word	nouilles	71
	in final syllable	grenouilles, citrouilles	71
ouls	in one-syllable word	pouls	69
oup	in one-syllable word	loup, coup, coup d'état,	ix, 69, 70, 112
		coup de pied	70
	in final position	beaucoup	70, 112
our	in one-syllable word	jour, pour, four, tour	71
	in final position	amour	71
ourd	in one-syllable word	lourd	71
ourds	in one-syllable word	lourds	71
ours	in one-syllable word	fours, jours, tours, ours	71, 72
ous	in one-syllable word	vous, sous, tous, fous,	ix, 70
		nous	70
	in final syllable word	dessous	70
out	in one-syllable word	tout	70
	in final position	debout, partout, surtout	70
oût	in one-syllable word	coût, goût, août	70
	in final position	dégoût, ragoût	70
oux	in one-syllable word	toux, houx, poux, doux	70
	in final position	époux, jaloux, genoux	70
oyer	in final position	foyer, loyer	79
	in infinitives	**employer, envoyer,**	78
		nettoyer, noyer,	78
		tutoyer, vouvoyer	78
oyez	in final position	vous employez	79
	in verb forms	(**employer**),	78
		envoyez (**envoyer**),	79
		nettoyez (**nettoyer**)	79
p	in initial position	papa, payer, pour	xi, 112
	in middle position	je romps (**rompre**)	113
	p in **mps**, **mpt** is	compte (**compter**)	113
	silent, mute (**muet**)	dompteur (**dompter**)	113
	in final position	hop, pop,	63, 113
	p is sounded	be-bop, stop	113
	in final position	coup, beaucoup	112
	p is silent, mute	galop, sirop, trop	63
	(**muet**)		
ph	in initial position	Philippe, photo	114
	in final position	photographie	114

Written Forms	Position in Word	Examples	Page Number
ps	**p** + **s** is sounded *ps*	psychologie, psychologique	114
		psychiatrie	114
q + ue	sounded *k*	que, quelle, question	114
		publique	102
		Québec	114
q + ui	sounded *kee*	qui	114
q + ua	sounded *ka*	quarante	xi
r	in initial position	raisin, raison, rue	xi, 115
	in middle position	harmonie, Paris	xi, 115
	in final position	cor, coeur, fleur	115
s	in initial position	silence, sur, soir	xii, 116
	in middle position	poison, désert	116
	in final position	pommes, femmes,	116
		livres, soeurs	116
		rose, ruse, cousin	116
ss	in middle and final positions	possible, massage,	117
		message, poisson,	117
		dessert, russe, coussin	117
		Claude Debussy	117
t	in initial position	tu t'es tu	120
		tutu, triste	xii, 120
	in middle position	tristesse	120
	in final position	petit, appétit, récit,	120
	t is silent, mute	elle finit (**finir**)	120
	(**muet**)	et, il est (**être**)	121
		elle dit (**dire**)	121
	in final position	dot, cet, net, Le Net	121
	t is pronounced	sept, huit, Zut!	121
		ouest, est, correct	121
tial, tie	**t** is pronounced **s**	prononciation, initial	121
tiel,	in endings **tion**,	partiel, démocratie	121
tieuse,	**tial, tiel, tie, tieux,**	ambitieuse	121
tieux,	**tieuse**		
tion			
th	**th** is pronounced **t**	thé, théâtre, théorie,	122
		thème, cathédrale,	122
		athlète, méthode,	122
		Théodore, Nathaniel	122
tone	in final syllable	monotone	90
u	in one-syllable word	tu, du, su, vu,	x, 10
		nu, nu-pieds	10
	in initial position, first syllable	utile, lutte, lune	10

Written Forms	Position in Word	Examples	Page Number
û	in one-syllable word	mûr, bûche	10
		sûr, dû	x, 20
ù	in one-syllable word	où	20, 69
ue	in one-syllable word	rue	x, 10
ueil	in final position	recueil, accueil	74, 75
ueils	in final position	recueils, accueils	74, 75
ueill	in initial position	cueilleur, cueillir	75
ueilles	in stressed position in verb form	tu accueilles (**accueillir**)	75
ueue	in one-syllable word	queue	x
ui	in one-syllable word	lui, huile, suis (verb form of **être**),	x, 84
			84
		nuit, huit	x, 84
	in first syllable	cuisine, juillet	84
	in final syllable	depuis	84
um	in final syllable	parfum	x, 88
un	in one-syllable word	un	x, 88, 94
	in initial syllable	lundi	88
ur	in one-syllable word	mur, sur, sûr	x
uyer	in final position	ennuyer, essuyer,	79, 84
		appuyer	84
v	in initial position	Vivienne, il (elle) veut	122
		(**vouloir**), viande, avant,	122
		vendredi	122
w	in initial position	week-end, whisky,	123
		western	123
	w is sounded **v**	wagon-restaurant	123
		wagon-couchettes, WC	123
x	as a single letter (*eeks* sound)	Madame X, Monsieur X	125
x	**x** + consonant	excellent, expertise	123
		extase, extravagant	123
	vowel + **x** + vowel	examen, exemple	124
		exercice, exister	124
	in final position **x** is silent, mute (**muet**)	heureux, cheveux	124
		chevaux, deux, beaux	124
	Exception:	phénix (**x** is sounded)	124
x + vowel	in middle position (*z* sound)	deuxième, beaux-arts	124
x + vowel	in initial position (*ks* sound)	xylophone, xérographie,	125
		xénophobie	125

Written Forms	Position in Word	Examples	Page Number
y	in initial, middle, or final position	allez-y, Vichy, cycle, cyclone, bicyclette	7 11 11
ya	in final position in initial position	Maya yaourt	79 79
yeux	one-syllable word final syllable	yeux joyeux, Joyeux Noël	x, 11, 83 80
yo	in middle position	mayonnaise	x, 3, 11, 83
yod	one-syllable word	yod	3, 11, 51, 54, 77, 78, 80, 83
you	in initial position in one-syllable word in final position	Yougoslavie youpi! voyou	80 80 80
yre	in one-syllable word	lyre	ix
z	in initial position	zéro, zèbre, zinzin zoo, Zut!	xii, 125 125
	in final position (see also **ez**)	allez, avez, ayez	48